Chrysalis

Chrysalis

The hidden transformation in the journey of faith

Alan Jamieson

Paternoster:
thinking faith

MILTON KEYNES ● COLORADO SPRINGS ● HYDERABAD

First published 2007 by Authentic Media
9 Holdom Avenue, Bletchley, Milton Keynes, Bucks,
MK1 1QR, UK
1820 Jet Stream Drive, Colorado Springs, CO 80921, USA
OM Authentic Media, Medchal Road, Jeedimetla Village,
Secunderabad 500 055, A.P., India
www.authenticmedia.co.uk
Authentic Media is a division of IBS-STL U.K., limited by guarantee,
with its Registered Office at Kingstown Broadway, Carlisle, Cumbria
CA3 0HA. Registered in England & Wales No. 1216232. Registered
charity 270162.

British Library Cataloguing in Publication Data

A catalogue record for this book is available from the
British Library

ISBN 13: 978-1-84227-544-3

Cover design by fourninezero design.
Print Management by Adare
Printed and bound in Great Britain by J.H. Haynes & Co., Sparkford

For soul mates along the way,
especially for those who helped me begin
in the context of All Saints Anglican Church – Nelson.

Contents

Acknowledgements

Thank you to those who have told me their stories. Each journey of faith, told and heard, has opened sacred space. It is from these stories and from my own story that this account has been shaped.

I also want to thank Andrew Willis and Becky Holmes who edited and reworked this text, Paul Fromont and Richard Hunt who read the first draft and suggested changes, and both the Dove Trust and Portland Trust (for information about the trust see www.portland.org.nz) which gave me the time to write.

Faith in an Emerging Culture
Series Preface

It is common knowledge that Western culture has undergone major changes and we now find ourselves in an increasingly postmodern (or post-postmodern?), post Christendom, post industrial, post-just-about-anything-you-like world. The church now sits on the margins of western culture with a faith 'package deal' to offer the world that is perceived as out of date and irrelevant. How can we recontextualize the old, old story of the gospel in the new, new world of postmodernity? How can we fulfill our missional calling in a world that cannot any longer understand or relate to what we are saying? 'Faith in an Emerging Culture' seeks to imaginatively rethink Christian theology and practice in postmodern ways. It does not shrink from being explorative, provocative and controversial but is at the same time committed to remaining within the bounds of orthodox Christian faith and practice. Most readers will find things to agree with and things which will irritate them but we hope at very least to provoke fresh thought and theological/spiritual renewal.

1

Butterflies – *transformation*

This book nearly had a different title. It could easily have been called *The Crucible*, after the cup-shaped containers used in laboratories to hold chemicals as they are heated to blistering temperatures. It would have been a good title: one that highlights the importance of being contained and held while the flaming heat of pain, disappointment and doubt are brought to bear on our lives and faith. And it would have held the submeaning of alchemy: that magical process whereby ordinary metals, heated together in a crucible, may become precious jewels, as base metals are transformed into gold.

In fact, it would have been an excellent title, for the hope of the crises of faith we encounter is that they are places where we change – and change for the better. The hope is that they are places where our sense of meaning is stretched, our faith grows and our intimacy with God deepens. But it would have made the transformation of faith seem magical – like alchemy – whereas Christian faith is an ordinary human journey, full of everyday choices and struggles, not magic.

In the end, I chose a different title: *Chrysalis*. It is a more organic title, with an image drawn from nature and deep Christian traditions, like the spiritual advice of St Teresa of Avila, to portray a radical and natural journey of transformation. The title points to the transformation in which a pupa becomes a caterpillar, a caterpillar a chrysalis and a chrysalis a butterfly: the one organism, with identical DNA, existing in quite different forms, transforming throughout its life. It is this organic, natural and radical image that parallels the journeys of Christian faith beyond their early beginnings into a maturity of selfhood, identity and depth: the journey from ordinary to saint. It is a journey of radical transformations and purposeful growth. And it is for ordinary people: people like us. It is for the people we know in our churches: people with ordinary jobs and real struggles. Often, it is also a scary and disorienting journey. It is a journey that is begun but not often completed. It is a journey too often aborted. It is a journey in which it is easy to get lost, for many crises of faith lead to bitter disappointment and to ceaseless destruction, rather than transformation. But it doesn't need to be like that. Crises of faith allow us to leave the past and find God in new ways. They can be transformational. This book is about these transformations. It will give an account of the journey of faith born out of Scripture, the best of Christian understanding throughout the centuries, the strength of research and psychology and the practical experience I can bring as a journeyer, a sociologist of faith and a pastor. The aim of this book is to offer hope for those who journey beyond the beginnings of Christian faith into the greater depths of God.

It was while driving through southern Ireland on the most idyllic of spring days that the idea of a chrysalis of faith entered my thinking. Sandra, my wife, had picked up a copy of a retreat centre brochure. The heading read 'Chrysalis' and the by-line – 'I often think of the peace and serenity of Chrysalis and remember the spirit of permission, a safe place for the internal me to tiptoe to the surface.'[1] Today many people need a chrysalis of faith: a protected place that allows for radical change to occur and from which a new, fragile true-self can emerge.

Hoped for readers

This book is primarily intended for people who want to make sense of their own journey of faith and particularly the crises they are experiencing along the way. It is for those who are filled with doubt, despair, disillusionment and pain, but it is also for those who are experiencing faith change devoid of any crises or suffering: for those who sense an awakening of their faith in new ways. And it is for those who want to understand or help support a friend through a difficult time. The book is also intended for pastors, ministers, spiritual directors, mentors and church leaders as a resource to give to people or as a guide in the companioning of people, especially in what I will call the chrysalis times of faith: the times of deep darkness and the worst deserts of faith. But, most importantly, this book is for people who find their faith changing and want to understand why.

This is not a book of research or theological debate. Such books are already readily available.[2] This is a practical book. It is an easy read. And it is an easy read that opens up insights about the difficult phases of Christian faith, using the life cycle of the caterpillar as a metaphor for our own journeys. Here, we will see the common progressions that have been understood by generations of discerning Christians before us.

Hopefully, this book will be a rough map on which to locate ourselves and the people we accompany in the journey of Christian faith. I say a rough map because it is not a topographical, or even a good road map, for such detailed maps do not exist for the journeys of the soul. Each person's journey is unique. No two journeys are the same. The best we can offer is a rough map like one of those tourist maps that has a few landmarks and key turning points on it, but no scale or detail. Or, perhaps, it is like a sketch that a friend might draw on the back of a bar mat to help us find somewhere we have never been before. In this vague sense the map can be helpful. A map reminds us that we are on a journey of faith, that we need to keep moving and it gives some idea of where we are and what might lie ahead.

Because it is a map with little detail, there is no point spending our energy focusing on map-reading. This is a journey to be lived and experienced. Although I love maps and am always keen to get one when we visit a new city, I am constantly amused by tourists who seem more transfixed by their map-reading than experiencing and enjoying the environment they are in. Tourists who are absorbed with map-reading are not actually present to their immediate surroundings. For tourists and faith journeyers, the whole point is to be present in the experience.

I remember hearing a story some years ago (I am afraid I don't know where it came from) of a tribe who lived at the base of a mountain. One day, one of their number climbed the mountain and came back to tell the villagers of his journey. He told them about climbing the foothills and finding enormous rivers that had to be crossed, and he explained where the best crossings were. He talked of climbing the steep cliffs and described rocky outcrops that marked the best approaches. He talked of cold nights and the equipment needed, of almost-hidden animal tracks that could be followed, of good campsites, and, finally, of the exaltation of climbing the last mountain spur. Then, having told the story a number of times, he headed off on other adventures. The villagers remembered the stories of the mountain climber. At night they would often recite them, describing in careful detail where the rivers were to be crossed and the cliffs climbed. They remembered rocky markers, great places to set up camp for the night and the beauty of the mountain-top scene. But, although they knew the story word-perfect, no one left the village and actually climbed the mountain.

This map, rough and incomplete, is for climbers. It is for those who undertake the demanding, yet fulfilling, journey to a deeper and deeper maturity of Christian living.

An epic journey

When I was younger, I used to look at people in their thirties and forties and wonder whatever changed for these people. They reached adulthood, formed their beliefs and world-views, and made commitments to family and vocation. 'Whatever changed for them?' I wondered. I could see the growing and changing nature of childhood very clearly. I could see the turbulent years of adolescence and secondary school and the liberating identity-forming period of young adulthood. But what happened after that? Did people change and grow further? Being young myself it was too easy to misunderstand physical changes to our bodies as the only form of growth. Of course, that illusion was far from the truth. Imperceptibly, at least spiritually and psychologically, enormous opportunities are opened to us for growth through our adulthood. This is an area that is becoming increasingly understood.

Our journey of Christian faith is a whole of life experience. It is an epic journey: more an ultramarathon than a quick sprint. Because it is a marathon, it is not all the same. For each of us, faith changes and develops. Sadly though, this is not how everyone understands it

In a survey of people's faith expectations, it was found that 65 per cent of people expected that faith should change and develop. Only 35 per cent of those surveyed expected faith to remain static or constant. When the responses were divided between those who attend church and those who don't, it was clear that these two groups had different expectations. Of those who attend church, 39 per cent felt faith should not change; of those who do not attend church, only 24 per cent felt faith should remain the same throughout life.[3] This means that people like me, who have spent years in the Christian church, are often surprised and ill-prepared if we come to a point where we sense our own faith changing, beginning to unravel or being undermined.

Yet, when we read the New Testament, we are reminded that we must move beyond childish ways and make the transition from drinking spiritual milk to eating solid food. Despite these reminders in Scripture, we are often shaken when our childish ways no longer 'work' as they used to, or we find ourselves choking on the solid food set in front of us.[4]

The epic journey of faith involves lots of change: and not simply surface changes, but tectonic-like shifts at the heart of our faith. It is often the very core nature of our faith that is changing but it is also about the whole of life. This is because faith is far more than a set of beliefs, a creed or a set of doctrines. The faith that Jesus modelled involves our whole intellect, our passions, our convictions and our willpower. It is an intrinsically relational endeavour. It is not something we could ever do, or could ever sustain, alone. As Frederick Buechner said, 'Faith is less a position *on* than a movement *toward*, less a sure thing than a hunch. Faith is waiting. Faith is journeying through space and time.'[5]

Faith is, after all, about making meaning out of our life experiences and living out of that context of meaning. All people everywhere, in all generations, have been meaning-makers. It is what people do. It is an – no, perhaps *the* – inherent characteristic of being human. This is the great genius of Victor Frankyl.[6] Frankyl, a psychiatrist, was imprisoned during the Second World War in the death camps of the Nazi regime. From his own experience and his observations of those who lived and those who died in the death camps, Frankyl showed that humanity's primary motivational force is the search for meaning. For 'faith is the activity of seeking and composing meaning in the most comprehensive dimensions of our experience.'[7]

Yet, Christian faith is also far more than just making meaning; it is living fully within the meaning we make. It is giving ourselves to living consistently with our deepest and greatest senses of meaning. This is what Jesus modelled: a life of faith comprised of meaning-making and meaningful living. The heart of his meaning-making was his utter trust in, and commitment to, the Father. His meaningful living was expressed in his bringing his Father's kingdom into the world.

Such an epic and all-embracing journey demands perseverance. If you have run a marathon, or travelled on an exhausting trip, you get some feeling for the perseverance needed in epic journeys. So too in the journey of faith.

Many people have written about this epic and lifelong journey of Christian faith. They have described how this meaning-making and meaningful-living core of our lives changes and develops throughout life. From a Christian perspective, this understanding of the journey of faith has been developed by ancient writers and mystics. Two of the key ones are St Teresa of Avila and St John of the Cross.

One of St Teresa's explanations of the Christian journey is of a progression through different rooms of a castle, as if it is a journey through a great house with each room holding new opportunities, struggles and learnings. St John of the Cross uses the analogy of a dark night and speaks of the dark night of the senses and the dark night of the soul as two discernible passages on the journey of faith. But it isn't only the great spiritual leaders who have described the journeys of Christian faith. In story form, so too did John Bunyan, in the classic novel *Pilgrim's Progress* and Hannah Hurnard, in her novels such as *Hinds' Feet on High Places*. Added to this is the growing theoretical understanding of stages of faith based on psychological research. Undoubtedly, the international leader in this work is Professor James Fowler of Emory University.

All the historical spiritual leaders, story-writers and psychological theorists of faith tell us that Christian faith is a dynamic, changing and evolving process, rather than something which is relatively static. For this reason faith is, perhaps, best described as a verb. In normal conversation we think of faith as a noun: something you have or don't have. But faith, understood as a verb, is a process of becoming. This process of becoming involves our loving, trusting, believing, acting, suffering, valuing, knowing and committing. In this sense, faith is more than an acceptance of certain statements of belief: it is a way of living which encompasses all of life.

While we will draw on the understanding of great historical Christian spiritual leaders, such as St Teresa and St John of the Cross and contemporary researchers, such as James Fowler and Sharon Parks, the dominant image I want to use is drawn from nature and inspired by the writings of St Teresa. She used the life cycle of a silkworm as a way of explaining how faith changes. She wrote:

> The silkworms come from seeds about the size of little grains of pepper ... when the warm weather comes and the leaves begin to appear on the mulberry tree, the seeds start to live, for they are dead until then. The worms nourish themselves on mulberry leaves until, having grown to full size, they settle on some twigs. There with their little mouths they themselves

go about spinning the silk and making some very thick little cocoons in which they enclose themselves. The silkworm, which is fat and ugly, then dies, and a little white butterfly which is very pretty, comes forth from the cocoon.[8]

We will not draw on the silkworm, but the very similar life cycle of the butterfly: the Monarch butterfly, in particular. As with all images, it has its limitations and, as with all analogies, it breaks down when pushed too far. Nevertheless, the life cycle of caterpillar to butterfly is a very helpful analogy from which to gain a new perspective on faith change.

Outside my childhood window, a swan plant grew. Each year, almost microscopic pupae appeared. From these most fragile of beginnings, tiny pyjama-striped creatures emerged and grew. Over successive months, multi-legged eating machines became boringly dormant chrsyalises. As a young child, I then lost interest in them and almost forgot them until that magical time when they began to emerge as butterflies. I was transfixed; I watched as they broke open the chrysalis and slowly unravelled their legs and wings, dried themselves in the sun. Then, tentatively at first but with growing confidence, they flew. Year after year, I watched the same sequence. Sometimes there were many caterpillars, big and fat. Sometimes there were just a few. One year, when the swan plants had few leaves, hardly any chrysalises hung from the branches. Sadly, there were times when injured and dead butterflies lay on the grass below.

Although I knew the sequence, I could see little resemblance between the beautiful butterflies that emerged and the spongy little caterpillars they had been. The journey of Christian faith is quite similar. It is a journey of almost imperceptible growth and radical transformations. It is a journey that many begin but few pursue throughout life. It is not that they give up; they simply set up camp at some point on the journey. They abandon the pilgrimage and become residents: lifelong caterpillars, or chrysalises, from which no butterfly ever emerges.

A joke in the Alpha study series concerns two caterpillars sitting on a leaf watching a butterfly flying past. As the two caterpillars watch, one says to the other emphatically, 'You'll never get me in one of those.' The one-liner reminds us that the life story of the caterpillar is one of major and significant change: so too are many people's journeys of Christian faith.

Caution

As with just about everything we buy these days, this book comes with a caution. Although it is shaped by the life cycle of butterflies (as I mentioned before, Monarch butterflies, in particular), we need to always be aware that human faith is far more complex than the journey of caterpillar-to-chrysalis-to-butterfly. While the phases of the butterfly lifespan provide an interesting analogy, the analogy is simply a scaffold to help make sense of a far more complex and varied number of pathways of Christian faith. Like James Fowler's stages of faith, the life cycle of the butterfly provides a potentially helpful image for understanding. The image can help to bring an awakening of understanding or the 'ah-ha' experience, as we see ourselves and our own faith journey being sketched through the stages of faith theory or the butterfly life cycle analogy. But, of course, we are more complex than theories and all analogies, no matter how illustrative, break down.

Unlike caterpillars and butterflies, we keep all our faith experiences and understandings within us. They remain part of us. More like Russian dolls than butterflies, the previous phases of faith are part of us and are alive deep within us. As Erik Erikson, the great guru of development theories, states: 'Each step is grounded in all the previous ones . . . and each step gives new connotations to all the "lower" and already developed stages as well as to the higher and still developing ones . . . this can never be said often enough.'[9] And, unlike the butterfly, our journey of faith into a chrysalis-like phase may be one we return to many times.

The caution we need to hold in our minds is that the butterfly analogy is helpful in seeing aspects of the pathway many Christians are beckoned into, but it is a simple analogy only. In the end, we are called to walk our own pathway: a pathway that is unique and personal into a deeper understanding and living out of our Christian faith.

2

Can't Get Enough – *growing*

He was so excited as he explained how much becoming a Christian had changed his life. Enthusiasm and gratitude were written all over his face. It was all exciting. It was a completely new start; a new life. And he was bubbling. He couldn't get enough. He wanted to be at every service, at every study group, at every prayer meeting and event the church had running.

Do you know the feeling? Was that you some years ago?

I have interviewed many people about their Christian faith, as part of research projects and spoken with many, many more as a youth leader and pastor. I have heard this story several times. Each time there are subtle differences and personal touches, but there are also these common themes: enthusiasm, a new beginning, a deep sense of belonging, the desire to be fully involved and that sense of not being able to get enough.

My own story is built around these same themes. I was one of those teenagers who became a Christian at a youth group camp and who rushed home to buy his own Bible. It was a paperback version of the Living Bible, complete with a hippy-styled cover and introductory notes on each of the books. I began by reading the Gospel of John, guided by the study booklet from which I'd prayed 'the sinner's prayer'. I became absorbed in youth group and church activities, outreaches, services, programmes and meetings. And I loved it. I was at most events early and left late. Sunday afternoons began with youth group in the late afternoon, which was a mix of Bible study, charismatic worship and faithful expectant prayer. This was followed by tea together, the evening service at the Anglican church we were part of and then supper at the vicar's place, with more singing and prayer that regularly went late into the night.

They were exciting days and not just for me. This was the dawning of the charismatic movement in New Zealand and we were riding the wave. A youth group that began with ten or twelve kids grew, in a few years, to a 120. It was the biggest youth group in the region and the envy of many vicars.

A few years later, I was living in another city and had joined one of the biggest churches in the country. It was a church that had almost died and could easily have been closed. But in the late 1960s, a new minister had arrived with the plan of staying a few years and then moving on to bigger and brighter possibilities. The church he inherited had less than twenty members, poor attendances, old buildings and little hope. Through prayer, a strong community evangelism programme and sustained expository preaching, the church began to grow. Again, riding the charismatic movement, the church took off. Over the next decade, attendances grew from a couple of dozen to over four hundred.

What attracted me was the preaching. Here was a church that made sense of Scripture in a relaxed, down to earth and everyday kind of way. The minister was someone who had a big vision of how the Christian faith could change the world. It became our home church for the next fifteen years. It was the church where Sandra and I were both baptized, in which we got married and later in which our children were dedicated. It was a church where we led the youth work for a number of years, led overseas short-term mission trips and it was the site of my training as a pastor. For eight of the fifteen years we were there, I was on the pastoral team as one of the church pastors. You couldn't get more involved or committed than we were. And we loved it. We couldn't get enough.

They were good years. They were years when we grew in our Christian faith. Everything was exciting and there were always new challenges ahead. My Bible reading moved from following daily notes in the gospels to reading great chunks of the Bible at a time. I would often read ten or more chapters a day. This led to leading Bible study groups, preaching and, eventually, studying for a degree in theology.

They were also years of real challenge and new commitments. My initial decision to follow Christ was followed by other, equally significant, conversions in the way I lived my life, in the decision to get baptized, in the decision to become part of the church leadership and a conversion of concern for the poor of the world and world mission. These conversions laid the ground for the costly conversion of doing the hard yards in the study of theology. Then, there was the big challenge of the potential move to full-time ministry on less than half my military salary and the personal and family costs of leading a growing church.

But there were also real doubts and significant hurdles. There were theological doubts, as university study threw up new questions about my Christian faith. There were intellectual doubts, as I was forced to grapple honestly with the persistent critiques and perceptive queries of close workmates and family. In addition, there were the doubts that cut far more deeply as significant leaders were shown to be living double lives, as people died despite our fervent prayers and as the reality of people's unanswered needs hit home.

Yet, through it all, we grew in our faith and we grew as people. It seemed like we would carry on growing in this way for many years to come. It seemed like this was what the Christian faith was about and the future would be like the present: growing and learning and being moulded by God in this way for the rest of our lives. Looking back, I greatly value what God led us through in those years. It was, to borrow from Watchman Nee, *The Normal Christian Life*. And it was very good.

But then it slowly began to lose momentum. We didn't move away from our faith or our roles in the church. We didn't disown God or break some moral code. We didn't hit questions that were unanswerable or decide the cost was too high and pull back. We simply came to the end of that way of being. If you have experienced the road of faith coming to a cul-de-sac like we did, then you know what we went through. If you haven't, you will probably struggle to accept what I am trying to say. For us, something changed. The very things we used to love and find encouraging in our faith and lives were now leaving us cold. What once seemed life-giving became stale and lifeless. And, despite trying to rev ourselves up to try harder, we found we could go no further.

Caterpillar Christians

In the early and normal phase of adult Christian faith our growth is primarily determined by, or at least is proportionally connected to, what we do. There appears a close correlation between Scripture reading, study, prayer, mission work and the growth of our faith. The more we do, the more we grow. This is the normal Christian life. This caterpillar-like phase is the phase of Christian faith that I will call 'conventional' or 'pre-critical'. This is the phase where growth is predictable and interconnected with our efforts.

Caterpillars emerge small and fragile as the shell of their pupae opens to a new world. When they open on a plant with plenty of green succulent leaves, they begin to eat. Caterpillars are eating machines that grow through consuming. This is what they do: they eat. And as they eat, they grow. Sadly, if a caterpillar is born to a poor, or non-existent, food supply, they will shrivel and die. They, like people of Christian faith, need good food to grow and develop. The pace and rate of their growth is determined, at least to some extent, by their consumption.

Like caterpillars, we too need to be wary of being exposed to those things that can destroy us. Jesus told a similar story, not about caterpillars but about seeds, to warn his followers of the dangers to their faith. In his parable, some seed fell on stony and unfertile ground, other seed fell on the path where the birds would come and snatch it and other seed fell in less fertile ground where it would grow so far and then be choked by thorns and weeds. In faith terms, the threats of greed, lust, laziness and self-indulgence circle us as much as the birds that fly over exposed seeds, or the spiders and other insects that lurk in search of caterpillars.

Despite these struggles for many Christian people, this phase of faith is personally very rewarding and from it they contribute greatly to their community and to people in need. They become the good seeds that grow into trees and from which great crops of fruit are found.

As caterpillars eat the swan plants they live on, they get bigger and bigger until their skin is stretched to breaking point. To grow further, they must shed layers of skin to make room for more and more growth. I wonder what this is like for the caterpillars. I don't know if caterpillars experience changes the way I do but, if I was a caterpillar, I suspect I would feel this was a scary and vulnerable experience – shedding one layer of skin to expose a new soft skin. Certainly, that is how I felt when I was awakened to new challenges and responded to the call to new commitments in my own faith.

When I was offered a training position as a pastor, it seemed a very big challenge to leave a secure job with a clear career path to head down the uncertain and very insecure path of training for pastoral ministry. Yes, it felt exactly like losing a secure and well-known skin and being exposed in a new, fragile way.

Comparing the normal adult experience of Christian faith to a caterpillar is not intended to demean in any way this phase of faith. It is crucially important. It is normal and to be greatly valued. For most people, this is the way they experience their faith. There are always new challenges, like the new skins of the caterpillar, and growth seems to follow a pattern of moving into a new area in which, at first, we feel very vulnerable. This vulnerability is followed by slow, incremental growth and a strengthening of that aspect of our faith. And then slowly comes the sense of being more secure – even of being fully stretched. At this point, we often find that a new challenge beckons with the implicit invitation to rid ourselves of an old skin, to shed that which is beginning to pinch and feel restrictive and to open ourselves to new possibilities of growth. For most of us, our Christian faith journey is a mix of growth and stagnation. There are times when we experience a ready appetite for Scripture, prayer and mission and there are times when we don't. That seems to be the way the Spirit of God is at work in so many people's lives. And for many, this process continues, unless there is a complete lack of appropriate food, a refusal to take on new challenges or accept new costs, or the birds of the air successfully undermine our Christian faith.

This 'normal' or 'pre-critical' phase of faith is most common for adult Christians. I call this phase of Christian faith 'pre-critical' because it is pre (before) the critical passage of adult faith maturation. St John of the Cross calls this critical passage of faith the dark night. I will liken it to the chrysalis transformation of a caterpillar into a butterfly.

Churches are full of adults whose faith is best described as 'pre-critical'. This should not be surprising, as this is why we have churches and congregations. They are places in which people can find some common faith identity, and a community of common faith to which they can belong. Often, during this 'normal', or 'pre-critical' phase of Christian life, identification with their church is a key identity marker for them. Most find enormous meaning and sustenance in their faith as they share in the activities of the church – worship, teaching, prayer and mission endeavours. Many experience a strong sense of belonging to their church community, which is often expressed as having 'an arrived feel to it', being 'at home' and providing a 'walled-in' commitment.[1] This phase of faith is very much a tribal phase, where being part of the tribe is powerfully significant to us. Here, the security of the tribe or the community of like-minded believers is important to our own beliefs, values and living. People in this phase of faith hold deep convictions and are often committed workers with a very strong sense of loyalty to the Christian faith and their church community.

The fact that for many caterpillars life ends at this phase is linked to the fact that for many Christians pre-critical faith is the form they are most comfortable with throughout their lives. There is tremendous richness and there are real strengths and great gifts linked with this phase of faith and yet, for some, it will not last, as they sense a beckoning into something new. They are beckoned towards an unknown, yet critical, transformation in their lives and faith.

When caterpillars have fully grown, filling out their last skin to the maximum, they often seem to get agitated. They begin walking all over their host plant, climbing up and down the stems as if ferreting around for something. This agitation marks the end of their eating. They are preparing for a change. Something unprecedented is ahead of them.

I felt this same kind of agitation as I came to the end of my theological training and became more competent and comfortable as a pastor. When it seemed that all I needed to do was keep on doing what I had been doing, I started to find prayer sterile, worship services irritating and much preaching (including my own) boring and disconnected from my life. The problem wasn't with my prayer life, the worship services or preaching. My prayer space wasn't changing, the worship services I attended were just as good, if not better than before, and the preaching was undeniably solid and sound. The problem was within me.

Over the last fifteen years, I have met many people who have experienced the same sense of agitation and dissatisfaction. It can drag on for months (even years) and only seems to grow and strengthen within us. Now, I realize this is a 'normal' part of Christian maturation. Back then, I thought I was losing my faith and that it must have been all my fault. So I, like so many others, tried even harder to pray, to join in with the worship, to focus more on biblical teaching. And all the time, I, the true self, was shrinking away on the inside. I became as agitated as the full-grown caterpillar crawling backwards and forwards, up and down their host plant. I was looking for something. I was restless, dissatisfied, agitated, frustrated and, if I was honest, downright angry. The words of the U2 song, 'I Still Haven't Found What I'm Looking For', became something of a personal mantra.

Now I realize this agitation can be the beginnings of something new. It can be the beginning of a transformation

of our selves and our Christian faith into a new
space. Now, I encourage people who sense a similar
ongoing and inexplicable agitation and restlessness to
relax and be still. I encourage them to see their agitation
as an invitation to explore what the Spirit is inviting them
into. It is time to explore their life and the life of Christ more
deeply. As Father Thomas Green suggests:

> There is no solid interior life except one which is grounded
> on a genuine, honest knowledge of myself and of Jesus Christ.
> We cannot love what we do not know. To love the Lord we
> must first come to know him in Jesus Christ. To love ourselves
> properly (which is also essential to any genuine spirituality) we
> must come to know ourselves as we truly are.[2]

It is a little easier to be still if we have some idea of what
may lie ahead. St Teresa gives us some hints from her own
experience of the life of prayer. She describes four stages of
prayer, in which she likens prayer to watering a garden. The
garden is our soul or life. It is already planted with flowers
and other plants which represent the virtues, gifts, abilities
and opportunities in our lives. The planting of the garden is
something that God has already done. Our task in prayer is
to water the flowers and plants in the garden. As we pray,
we are like a gardener drawing water for the garden. The
drawn water is our sense of the Spirit of God nurturing us.
St Teresa suggests that the stages of prayer are like different
methods of watering the garden. She wrote:

> It seems to me the garden can be watered in four ways. You
> may draw water from a well (which is for us a lot of work).
> Or you may get it by means of a water wheel and aqueducts in
> such a way that it is obtained by turning the crank of the water
> wheel. (... the method involves less work than the other, and
> you get more water.) Or it may flow from a river or a stream.
> (The garden is watered much better by this means because the
> ground is more fully soaked, and there is no need to water so
> frequently – and much less work for the gardener.) Or the water
> may be provided by a great deal of rain. (For the Lord waters
> the garden without any work on our part – and this way is
> incomparably better than all the others mentioned.[3]

The stages of prayer are not a strict progression of stages, but involve some overlapping and interconnection. Nevertheless, the early and normal method of prayer is like hauling water by hand: a task that is laborious and in which we receive little water for the effort put in. But it is also understandable. As we work in prayer to quieten our minds, to focus on the ways of God and are serious about our prayer life, we receive the reward of our labours in the presence of the Spirit, albeit often less of a sense of the Spirit than we would like. But then the well runs dry and we can either get agitated and angry about it or accept the invitation to water the garden in new ways.

The agitated caterpillar is in a very similar situation. Sooner or later, it must stop wandering and begin to weave a small silk pad that will act as an anchor point for the caterpillar to hold onto as it hangs upside down and awaits what will happen next.

3

Golden Crucible – *cocooning*

Why do caterpillars stop eating and start weaving the silk anchor point from which their chrysalises will hang? Why, when there are more leaves to eat, do they simply choose to ignore them? What compels them to start shedding the last layer of skin as they hang upside down – waiting? How do they know that it is time to cease consuming and begin creating? How do they design and build their cocoon? And why is it that some caterpillars keep on eating and crawling along their host plant, when others are well into chrysalis formation?

Like birds who suddenly decide to stop nesting and start epic journeys southward for the winter, something triggers the caterpillars' radical change in behaviour. But what is it?

Probably, like birds beginning to fly south, the impulse of the caterpillars to start weaving is a mix of internal instinct and external cues. As the weather begins to change, something triggers an internal knowing that it is time to stop what they have been doing and set off in a new direction. Yet, it is such a radical change of behaviour that it seems incongruous.

For some people, the journey of faith is very similar. Inexplicably, they find themselves no longer wanting to do the very things that have sustained and nurtured their faith for years, perhaps even decades. People who have found services of worship encouraging and something that sustains their faith can find themselves disgruntled with the worship services, perhaps even turned off by them. Others who were most encouraged through listening to sermons and reading theology find that they are bored and disinterested. Still others, who sensed they were closest to God in prayer or when they were involved in serving others, find they can no longer pray or serve with any integrity. It is not that the worship has necessarily changed, the preaching standard declined, or their prayer times or care of others altered. It is simply that they are not connecting with it personally. Like the caterpillar that finds it no longer has an appetite for eating, it can't be explained simply by looking at the quantity or quality of green leaves available.

Of course, we all have times when the very things we find most rewarding in our Christian faith and the things that seem to connect us most strongly with the Spirit of God leave us cold. That is normal. But, when we have tried hard to connect, and the sense of disconnection and alienation only seems to strengthen, it may be an invitation to something completely new. This is particularly possible when even the very best preaching, worship, prayer times and opportunities in mission or service create only a continued sense of disinterest and dissatisfaction. It may be time to look in a new direction when, no matter what we try doing, we still know deep within that it is not working. While an individual's sense of dissatisfaction is always personal and unique, it often includes a very strong sense of two or more of the following.

- **Disenchantment:** this is the sense of not enjoying activities of faith that have previously been very personally rewarding.
- **Disillusionment:** this is the sense that for differing reasons they feel let down, sad, perhaps cynical, and often quite destructive in their view of their faith, the faith of others and, maybe, church. What was once life-giving, now feels life-less and they can wonder if, after all, they are wasting their time. With disillusionment comes a disengagement from church.
- **Disengagement:** this is the sense that they feel they are no longer connected, interested or involved in what is going on in the church, its structures and its direction, or within the church community.

- **Disidentification:** this is the sense that they no longer identify with the church, the activities, the worship and the people there and begin to observe as an outsider would.
- **Disorientation:** this is the sense that they don't know where they belong any more. This is often coupled with a sense of having lost their bearings, their anchor, and, perhaps, even their identity. Sometimes, the sense of disorientation is linked to feelings of loss and uncertainty, and, with it, a new anxiety can creep in. Typically, this is also linked to a sense of freedom, curiosity about the future, and excitement about possibilities ahead.[1]

At this time we are most aware of what isn't nurturing our faith any more and what we want to stop doing or get away from. Gerald May, in his very helpful book *The Dark Night of the Soul*,[2] takes this sense of dissatisfaction further, saying:

> A common experience, often confusing but not too painful, is that the word of 'God' loses its meaning. That word, which used to bring forth images and feelings, now seems inadequate and somehow even wrong. And there seems to be no satisfactory substitute … A much more unsettling experience is the loss of the sense of God's presence, which can often feel like being abandoned by God. Many people are used to a consistent and long-lasting feeling of the presence of God in their lives. It may be a distinct sense of presence, of companionship everywhere. It may happen more in relationship with children, spouse, or other beloved people. It may occur in special places, as in church or outdoors in nature. Even more often it is just too subtle to describe at all. Whatever form it takes, however, it is sensible, palpable, and deeply meaningful. Then, sometimes, it disappears.

Accompanying our dissatisfaction may be a very quiet yearning from deep within us for something completely new. A story may help to try and explain what this change in our faith journey feels like. This story came to me while on summer holiday near a beautiful beach about eleven years ago. It was my first attempt to make sense of what I personally had been feeling.

Imagine going to a beach for the first time and observing people swimming and playing in the water. They seem to be enjoying themselves enormously and are obviously proficient at swimming. After a while you get to know some of the swimmers and they offer to teach you to swim so you too can enjoy the water. Seeing what they have, encourages you to join them. Swimming turns out to be a great success and for the next few years you enjoy swimming at the beach as part of the club. Eventually you become a swimming instructor yourself. You are challenged by the opportunity to help others learn to swim between the flags and enjoy the sea as you have learnt to do.

One day, standing on the beach, you wonder what it would be like to swim further, or to go exploring the rock edges, or maybe to dive to the depths of the bay, out beyond the flags. The yearning to stretch out beyond the beach doesn't simply go away, but appears to get stronger and builds within you. Around the same time, you notice that you are becoming increasingly self-conscious about going swimming. It doesn't seem as important, or as much of a challenge as it used to be. Thinking about this, makes you realize you don't enjoy the swim club like you used to and you're becoming critical of all the swimming and playing near the beach. But then, socializing with a group of deep-sea fishermen each weekend and hearing their stories of fishing trips adds fuel to your desire to go beyond the flags. As time drifts on, dislike turns to resentment and you tentatively mention to some of the others at the beach your desire to go beyond the flags. The coach gets to hear of your comments and warns you of the dangers of swimming outside the flags. He tells stories of people who went out there and have never come back. Instead, he suggests that you go to a swimming gala to rekindle your enthusiasm.

The swimming gala seems to do the trick – at least, for a while. But then, standing on the beach one day, the yearnings return. This time they are even stronger than before. On swim days you find it harder and harder to get yourself out of bed and are aware of making all sorts of excuses as to why you shouldn't swim that day. One swim day you wake up realizing you haven't been to the beach for three or four months. You wonder what to do next. Should you go back or not? Eventually you come to the conclusion you don't ever want to go back again. All you do there is swim backwards and forwards and play in the waves. It was fun, even exciting for a number of years, and you thought swimming was all there was to life: but not now. Now you want more. Of course, you remain a swimmer; after all, no one can deny your experience of the sea. But you're rarely seen at the beach between the flags. It is time to push out into the deep. It is like when Peter and the disciples had been fishing all night in the relative shallows, and then Jesus came along and asked them to push out into the deep; and it was there that they caught the surprising catch.[3]

Why do some people become dissatisfied with the swimming between the flags, or need to be called into the deep? I don't know the answer. Equally, it is hard to explain why some people become dissatisfied with the ingredients of faith (maybe even church) that have been so good for them for so long. Like the caterpillar that decides to stop eating and start weaving, the swimmer who wants to leave the safety of swimming within the flags to go scuba diving, or the bird that leaves the nest to begin an epic journey, it is a mix of an internal desire, instinct, compulsion or need, and external triggers. What is clear is that continuing to do what we have always done is no longer helpful. The more we try, the more we become alienated, dissatisfied, and even angry.

Internal motivators

Often the first major shift we sense is one from dependence to counter-dependence.[4] This occurs when, for a sustained period of time, the faith activities we have depended upon to grow and strengthen our Christian faith become the very things that we most strongly push away from. We do this because we have become bored by them; or worse, we have become irritated and angry by them. When we are approaching a significant faith transformational period of the same magnitude as the caterpillar beginning to weave its chrysalis, the harder we try doing the same things and the stronger our dissatisfaction becomes. In the end, we realize we are fighting ourselves.

At this point, the natural response is to find someone to blame. Two possibilities loom largest: either we blame ourselves, or it is the fault of others, the preacher, the minister, those who lead the worship, prayer and mission programme. Blaming ourselves may lead us to try harder, or to try to ignore our negative responses, or to try a new method, or to simply give up as we blame ourselves for not having what it takes. Sadly, this is often the advice that 'friends' and Christian leaders tend to give us. 'Try harder,' they say; or, 'Go on this training course.' 'Listen to this new speaker,' they say; or, 'Read this new book.' Some may even blame us personally, suggesting our present situation is an indication of sin in our lives, a lack of faith, or an unwillingness to be fully committed. It is all well-meaning advice but, ultimately, unhelpful. It is as unhelpful as Job's advisors as he struggled with why God had seemingly deserted him.

On the other hand, blaming the church or mission group structures, leaders, programmes and agendas, rarely changes the underlying dis-ease. Many people, particularly those in leadership positions, try to change the way things are done at this point, in the false hope that doing so will provide them with what they need and be more helpful for others. If they are successful and changes are made, they tend to find that their own enthusiasm for the new changes is very short lived and few others seem interested. The simple fact is that at this point, people are far more aware of what they don't want than of what they do need. Changing the externals doesn't assist the much deeper budding of a new core structure to their faith and lives.

There is, understandably, someone else we can blame: God. For those of us brought up in the Christian faith, blaming God, going so far as cursing God, is an anathema. Yet it is very biblical.

The Old Testament journey of Job can be helpful as a rough guide to what lies ahead. In the opening verses of the book of Job we meet a man who has been blessed by God and has a firm foundation of faith. He is a man with a scrupulous concern for sin and a fear that either he or one of his children could fail God. Here is someone who both God and Satan could agree was very good. Job is a man who sees the Lord's presence in the good things that he has been given, like his farm, house, family and health and he acknowledges them as blessings. Yet despite Job's faith, thankfulness and scrupulous focus on remaining sinless, he is nevertheless taken through a horrendous unpicking of his faith. In effect, he hits the wall: the wall where faith is dislocated. Job is thrown into a new and confusing world. The old trust in the beliefs of the time is now replaced with unanswered questions and deep doubts.

Although his friends remind him of the orthodox teachings of the community of faith, he cannot accept them. They simply do not connect with his new experience of life. He can no longer accept that the sickness and suffering he experiences could be warranted by his failings. He doesn't claim to be perfect but that his present suffering is not deserved. The formula of faith which stated that sinfulness is the cause of suffering doesn't make sense. Job's confidence in the beliefs and teaching of the community of faith has been usurped by his own internal authority which tells him their formulas don't work. Throughout the book, there is an increasing self-confidence which gives Job the courage to disagree with his friends and rail against God. God had been present to Job through blessings. But now, only the absence and silence of God remains. A life previously built on the beliefs and teaching of faith is overwhelmed by the pain and reality of his experience: an experience that speaks with new truth and disqualifies the answers of the past. This is the second phase of Job's journey; it is a phase dominated by doubt and questions, by anger and disappointment with God. Job's confidence in his lived experience is now much stronger than past convictions and the recipes of faith offered by others. It is a time of critically unpacking his faith and of an angry search for the God who seems to have disappeared.

Looking back at Job reminds us that for many, the internal dis-ease in our Christian faith is intimately connected to significant personal suffering, grief and pain. While some may approach a significant faith reorientation because of a natural opening to a new stage of life, others are propelled into it by intrusive life events, like the death of a loved one, illness, serious accident, the loss of a job, a broken relationship or dashed dreams. For others, it is driven more by internal motivators, as a restlessness for something more sets in. These internal motivators may be simply a quiet, persistent unease, or they may be a much stronger stirring in the form of stress, burnout, a chronic sense of exhaustion, an addiction that can no longer be ignored, unhealed wounds from the past, or an eruption of doubt or fear.

These internal drivers are the most significant and deeply felt motivators to push us on a new soul journey, but they are often influenced and connected with contextual changes. So we also need to be aware of the influence of our wider context. Clearly, birds that migrate and caterpillars that cease eating to begin weaving are responding to internal instincts; but they are also influenced by changing weather patterns. So too are we. There is a wider context that influences the way we make sense of and live out our faith.

External triggers

The nature of society is radically changing. In western societies like New Zealand, the way of living and doing church as it was in the 1950s has largely gone because somewhere between 1960 and 1980 a 'new world' began to emerge. Sociologists talk of modernity and postmodernity to name the shift that has occurred. Too often, though, explaining what they mean by postmodernity seems to lose the layperson in a cloud of imprecise academic concepts. As the Canadian Sociologist David Lyon commented in his text, aptly titled *Postmodernity,* 'The very notion that we can build up progressively towards a complete or – heaven help us – total view of postmodernity would be an anathema.'[5] It is, however, possible to talk of some key changes that, taken together, drive the move into postmodernity. Sociologists talk of five such key changes in particular.[6] I have found that explaining these key changes helps people to see the impact of societal changes on their own more personal faith journey.

A distrust of meta-narratives, experts and authorities creating a crisis of meaning

The so called period of 'modernity' can be dated from around 1789 to 1989.[7] These two dates point to two significant world events that symbolize both the beginning and the end of the modern era. In 1789 'the French Revolution decisively dethroned God and proclaimed the arrival of the secular state'.[8] The revolution marked the end of the pre-modern period where God and God's providence and the world of the supernatural were seen as intimately involved in the 'real' world of everyday people. The underlying acceptance of God and of God's providence and care was replaced with progress: human progress through a trust of the senses, rationality and science.[9] In other words, one grand explanation of the world and life was replaced by another. That is, one 'meta-narrative', or 'big-story', replaced another. So the big framework based on God and God's providence, care, judgement and leading was replaced by a growing trust in a framework based on human progress, the knowledge of science, trust in rationality and the hope of a better, human-made world.

The fall of the Berlin Wall in 1989 marked the end of European communism and the beginning of postmodernism in which an 'incredulity towards meta-narratives' became increasingly shown, not only in people's distrust of all big stories and overarching frameworks, but also in growing distrust of authority figures and experts. The previously foundational institutions of religion, royalty and tradition were increasingly undermined. The net effect has been an unprecedented destruction of meaning.

A loss of belief in progress creating a crisis of hope

The reasons for the loss of belief in progress are numerous, but several are raised most consistently including: the impact of two world wars; the horrors of the Nazi extermination of the Jews; the Vietnam war; a litany of self-serving political decisions by key leaders (e.g. Watergate); the degradation of the environment, and the realization that as science and technology expanded the suffering of the world seemed to increase. Despite our technical ability to feed the world and deal with most world health issues, human poverty has actually increased. The technologies that previous generations saw as the hope of the future have not solved perennial world problems but have, in fact, created new problems: for example the impact of modern technology and science on the world environment. The net result is a lack of hope in human progress.

A move away from institutions creating a crisis of identity and belonging

While we hear everywhere of the demise of sports clubs, community groups, political parties and churches, due to lack of members, we too often miss the impact of fundamental change in two key institutions that have framed belonging for decades – work and family. In western societies, these core institutions have become far more fluid. My parents' expectation of working within one career and, probably, for one, or at most two or three, employers, has given way to an expectation that during our working lives, we will need to have multiple careers and several employers. Loyalty between employer and employee has significantly changed to the point that workers no longer expect the same loyalty from their employer and employers know that employees are likely to move on when a better offer comes their way. The fluid nature of the career and employment environments affects both people's sense of identity and belonging. Added to this is the fluidity of family structures. With increasing numbers of divorces and second and third marriages, partnerships, de facto relationships and blended families, it can seem almost as if every extended family gathering is a new event, as new people are included and others are absent. Again, people's sense of identity and belonging is impacted as the enduring strength of family bonds declines.

A move from a production-driven economy to a consumption-driven economy creating a crisis of debt

While capitalism and the power of the financial markets have only continued to grow in influence over recent decades, the core, driving engine of capitalism has markedly changed. Where modern capitalism was driven by production, postmodern capitalism is driven by consumption. The underlying rationale behind capitalism, often called the Protestant work ethic, was that people worked hard and, instead of spending their earnings, they saved as much as possible and invested their savings for the future. It was an ethic of delayed gratification. Today, capitalism operates on exactly the opposite ethic; people are encouraged to buy what they want now and finance it through increasing debt. An enormous marketing and advertising industry has grown up alongside this core shift in the essential nature of economies, not so much to inform people of potential products, but to create a desire and hunger for numerous products and services we don't need. Pleasure, once seen as the enemy of capitalism, is now an essential element.

A rather tongue-in-cheek explanation of this shift has been described by changing Descartes' maxim, '*I think, therefore I am*' to a view of society in which, '*We are what we consume.*' It is not simply that we live in a world of theme parks, shopping malls, TV commercials and junk mail; we live in a world where 'consumerism' itself dictates in education, health, religion, sport and leisure. Through the power of the international shares, currency and futures markets the impact of consumerism is global. This does not mean that everyone enjoys the 'consumer lifestyle'; in fact, there are many who don't, but everyone is undoubtedly affected by it.

*An explosion of communication technology which creates a
crisis in the relationship of space and time*

Part of our planning for a recent church service involved asking
people to bring objects that reflected their daily life contexts.
One of our very old members told me that he was going to
bring something that represented the way he communicates
with people today. He went on to describe learning Morse
code when he first began work on the railways. It was the
only way of communicating from one station to the next.
Now in his nineties and quite computer literate he can email
people around the world, call them on a cell phone or access
information on just about anything from his home computer.
This is a phenomenal shift in communication capabilities
during one lifetime. Communication technology, which
we take for granted, affects our sense of time and space,
increasingly making us an instant society that expects to be
able to get anything, from anywhere, now! Communication
technologies affect our sense of space as they bring us into
multiple contexts simultaneously. A few years ago I was in
Norway speaking to my family in Wellington, New Zealand,
on a mobile phone, while simultaneously watching live TV
coverage of a bomb attack in the Middle East which was
being commented on by a broadcaster in the United States.
In that one moment I was 'live' in the real-time happenings
on four different continents.

These five postmodern streams are combining to create what
sociologists are calling a liquid society. The old fixed and
solid society is giving way, they argue, to an increasingly
fluid society. The change in our cultural situation could
be viewed as similar to devastating floods, with the only
difference being that the flood cutting across our cultural
landscape shows no sign of easing. In fact, the waters simply
keep rising, as old structures are weakened and people are
forced to live in radically different ways.

The metaphor of streams combining to form a raging flood
is helpful for our understanding and sense of appreciation
for the 'postmodern'.

Living in this emerging 'liquid'[10] world is, metaphorically, like leaving the dry land to travel with the raging river and like being carried by its currents, ebbs and flows in ways quite different from life on solid ground. In the church setting, this theme has been picked up by Pete Ward in his book *Liquid Church*[11] and extended by Len Sweet and Darryl Dash, who are calling the coming context that faces the Christian church not just a liquid reality, but *The Perfect Storm.*[12]

As individuals and churches, we increasingly find ourselves caught in this liquid world. It is a turbulent context of great change, as we move between two worlds: one that is dying and another that is ready to be born. In this time of death and birth, we face enormous turbulence. Anne Deveson states, 'Somehow – in the immediate future – we had to find the courage and wisdom to radically change our whole way of living and being.' She quotes John Maynard Keynes, 'The real difficulty lies not in developing new ideas, but in escaping from old ones.'[13] 'It's not enough to adapt within the norms of the past. We need to discover profoundly new ways of perceiving the world in which we live.[14]

Within this broader context, increasing numbers of people are being prompted by changing external factors to move beyond a 'pre-critical' framework of Christian faith. And when this external contextual change coincides with internal promptings of the Spirit, they become increasingly hard to ignore. Like birds drawn to migrate and caterpillars propelled to begin weaving, we are being asked to become something new.

But leaving behind the old familiar ways and contexts of faith is also scary and we tend to stay where we are until the pain of staying where we are becomes unbearable. As Alan Jones states:

> It seems to be a maxim of the Spiritual life that no-one undergoes spiritual or psychological growth and change *willingly*. We are either dragged into it kicking and screaming, or circumstances force us into the next scene of the human comedy. Ironically, the institutional church is often an obstacle to spiritual growth … it has something of an investment in keeping its members in an infantile state[15]

Yet the move into this transition cannot be rushed, pre-empted or pushed. We can no more rush a caterpillar from eating to weaving than we can push ourselves, or someone else, into a crisis or transformation of faith. Ultimately there is mystery here. And around this mystery hang many questions. Some of those questions are: Why do some people never move to the edges of a pre-critical faith phase? Why do some people begin a faith transition and then go no further? Why does pain and suffering, disappointment and loss, personal failure or serious critical study propel some into the beginnings of a faith transformation? Why do the exact same events leave another person's pre-critical expression of faith stronger? While we can attempt to answer these questions by talking about global changes to society and personal life experiences, we can't predict or perceive the internal work of the Spirit. It is simply a mystery.

That said, some people come to this seismic faith shift and some don't. We must remember what Kester Brewin says, 'It is no good egging someone on . . . what is important is that the path is clear for them to travel when they find their way there in their own time. In fact, it would be criminal to force people on before they were ready.'[16]

At this point, we have no idea what lies ahead. There is only the loss of the known and the secure and a dark, unknown and unmapped future. It is a very disorienting and frightening place in which to be. This is a crisis of faith. We can no longer stay where we are. We must leave this way of understanding and living our faith behind but what lies ahead is, at best, misty. What we do know is that the cocooning process is always a process of grief, and a loss of the known and the familiar. Whatever lies ahead, we can be sure that grief will be involved. This time of cocooning will include at least some of the following – shock and anger, denial, and the need for open spaces for despair and silence. No wonder we prefer the familiar to the possible!

The chrysalis time is a time of transformation and we cannot transform ourselves. This is the Spirit's work. Yet the Spirit works in partnership with us. On our part, we need to be prepared to surrender to the Spirit's work and be willing to do the hard emotional and spiritual work required of us. Most often, we find ourselves entering this chrysalis time because we can do nothing else. We have been brought to our knees by our own incapacity, by failure, by suffering, or through being drawn into the adventure of entering the unknown.

Recently I had coffee with someone at exactly this point. I had been speaking at a conference on the faith development of young adults and was due to fly home. There was little time between the end of my sessions and the timing of my flight. One of the people at the conference offered to drive me to the airport, saying as she did, 'I have forty minutes with you before your flight; tell me everything you can about what I should do next.' With this introduction she explained that she and her husband had been part of the same church for more than a decade. Over recent years she had found herself increasingly alienated within it. It simply wasn't where she was at any more. But she was passionate about her faith and her work. She had tried staying for many months, well beyond the point that she was personally getting anything out of it or was able to productively contribute within it. In the past, she had been a significant leader; she had even been approached about being employed on the pastoral staff. Her husband also needed to leave but her children, now teenagers, were involved and it was an environment where their faith was growing. She had tried explaining to the pastor what she was feeling and he had interpreted it as a form of rebellion and lack of faith on her part. He had explained to the leadership that she was in a stage of rebellion.

As the airport approached, she explained that she didn't want to lose her faith. God was very important to her and she wanted to strengthen her faith and continue to serve God, but she couldn't stay in the kind of church context that had been their spiritual home for so long. She was scared what might happen if they were to leave. She had friends who had left and it seemed their leaving had led to a loss of faith. They had got involved in living it up, had had affairs and 'it all got very messy'. This is not what she wanted for herself or her family. What should she do?

Having checked in, and with a few minutes to spare, we sat down for a coffee. What should she do? She needed to hear and trust her own internal truth. If she stayed in that church, or did the same style of things at another, similar one, it would only become increasingly unhelpful, even toxic, for her. I talked about people whom I had interviewed who had tried staying on and staying on to the point they had headaches or nausea as each Sunday approached. These people became so angry inside as they dragged themselves through the doors that they were toxic to those around them. It was time to leave. The diet of the church wasn't going to nurture her in the next phase of her journey and the leadership and pastor were not going to be able to support and accompany her. Staying on would only make it worse for herself, her family and those with whom she met. But if she left, what lay ahead? All she could see was a big hole and very real dangers: the dangers of losing her faith or of going down a track similar to those she had seen leave before her.

We talked about the next phase probably being an intensely personal and, at times, lonely phase. But it would be a time when the Spirit of God would be meeting her in new ways, drawing her inwards to sense, listen to and strengthen her own inner identity, truth, wisdom and contribution. Alongside this we talked about the need for a companion through this phase: someone like a spiritual director who could provide a safe place for her to tell her story. She needed someone who would understand and be able to respect and honour her questions and doubts, allowing her space to explore her own way forward and validating her own sense of truth and knowing. She needed someone who could introduce her to new symbols, metaphors and images of Christian faith and God. She needed someone who could suggest new ways of prayer and approaching Scripture, who would be a companion as she perceived her own giftedness and sense of vocation, and who would be alongside as new fragile ways of living and being with God began to bud and take root.

We talked about a person who could provide this kind of support for her, whose personal faith she admired, who had walked through their own dark nights and faith crises, and who could truly accompany her. Together they would weave the chrysalis space that she needed to hold and protect her as her faith began to be transformed.

Then we talked about other specific ways in which she might invest the time and energy that was once given to church services, leadership and involvement, because it isn't just a matter of stopping one way of doing faith. We stop one activity in order to give ourselves to the new things God is bringing to life within us.

She needed to leave her church as part of this journey. I suspect that most people don't need to break their ties. An increasing number of ministers, pastors and leaders are aware of the changing nature of faith and are able to accommodate, validate and even support people as they move through them. Certainly, the importance and role of church activities may decrease in significance for a period of time, but this may not need to lead to leaving. Often, for family reasons, it is easier to remain part of the church, even if for this time our level of involvement may be quite small.

I have studied and supported church leavers for over ten years now. In that time, I have heard more than a thousand stories of people moving through faith crises: people young and old, men and women, from Norway to New Zealand. Having heard their stories and having accompanied these people, my advice would be: if you have a church base where you have been significantly involved and if you are able to maintain nominal links while you move into the next phase of faith that God is opening up to you, then do so.

Only leave if you really can't stay. Only leave if staying is becoming toxic to your faith and life. Learn from the caterpillar that attaches itself to the plant that it has lived on to this point; it weaves a silk anchor point on the very plant it has depended upon as a food source, but no longer needs. As we enter this time of radical transformation, we too need to hang securely independent from, but nevertheless relationally linked to, a community of faith.

While I encourage people to stay a part of their faith community, if it is possible to do so, I also encourage them to focus their energy on the transformation and growth of their own faith, not the direction of the church. Recently, I found my perspective on this point being debated on a blogsite discussion. A writer responded to my advice that 'now is not the time to try and change the church', by describing it as troubling. In reply the writer said:

> My consuming passion, my zeal and fire all revolve around changing the church. All my research, my theology, my debating, my dreaming and my waking, my wrestling in prayer, my flirting with depression: it all comes back to my unshakeable belief that the church needs to change both theologically, methodologically and culturally, and my perceived sense of vocation to be part of that change. Yet as I read Jamieson's words of caution, I sense and suspect that he is perfectly correct. Now is *not* the time for me to be changing the church. Right now I am like someone who has tried to change a building with a chainsaw, sledgehammer, and dynamite, all to no avail, and am left kneeling beside its unscathed bluestone wall, hammering on it with my fists, and crying out through my own tears 'change, damn you, change!'
>
> Maybe now is not my time for me to change the church. But if that is not what 'now' is about, then what is[17]

All I can say in response is that what is emerging at this transitional phase in your faith is vastly different to all that has gone before. It is as different as chalk and cheese. Something unique, important, unprecedented and essential is beginning to happen. This transition has the same significance as when the caterpillar ceases to eat and starts to weave that anchor point from which their chrysalis will hang. Through all this radical upheaval and change we can be encouraged to remember that the Greek word for chrysalis means gold.[18] This transition, which we are entering, can open up ways for the Spirit of God to bring new things into our lives that are as precious and priceless as gold.

So the caterpillar stops wandering, begins to spin the little silk pad on the underside of a leaf or branch and then turns around and grabs hold of that silk pad with its hind legs. Once it is securely hooked onto the silk pad, the caterpillar drops down, suspended by its back legs, trusting the silk pad to secure it. Then it begins to change form; in technical terms, it begins to metamorphose.

4

In the Dark – *letting go*

The dark days are just beginning. Before you emerge into the light again you will be stripped to the core. You will rage and scream at God. You will retreat into a cocoon of sorrow and breathe in slow motion. The colour will drain from the sky, the meaning from life. As a plough tears through hard earth, your heart will be broken up. You will make friends with pain, nursing it as the child of grief. Utter emptiness fills the earth, and the valley appears to contain nothing but the echo of your own cry. Surely God has left you. The road which seemed to be heading somewhere has become a dead end. A mocking maze with no exit.

Then, one morning in the distant future, you wake and hear a bird singing ...

Mike Riddell[1]

A dark night now approaches. It is too soon to listen for birdsong. Now is the time of darkness. It is a time for stillness and silence. A process is beginning; in fact, it begins for a caterpillar while it is still busy eating. Imperceptibly, internal changes are already beginning to happen under the skin of the caterpillar. Outwardly, the caterpillar looks exactly the same, but under the skin a chrysalis has begun to form. When the caterpillar attaches itself to its anchor point and hangs upside down, its last skin begins to split and fold back; as it does so, what is revealed is not another layer of skin but something quite new: a chrysalis. The caterpillar has entered a new phase of growth; a phase of stillness and darkness.

St John of the Cross is the great teacher about the chrysalis times of faith. He called these times dark nights. He teaches us that when despair and suffering, doubts and questions, evil and even, ultimately, death face us, there is no point trying to run away. The darkness is real and we must go into it. We must face this new darkness squarely. For St John of the Cross and St Teresa the darkness is not to be feared, but rather, it is a space that gives new meaning, purpose and energy to our faith. As Gerald May says, 'The dark night of the soul, in John's original sense, is in no way sinister or negative. It is, instead, a deeply encouraging vision of the joys and pains we all experience in life. It inspires the desire to minimize suffering and injustice wherever possible, and at the same time it sheds a hope-filled light on the pains that cannot be avoided. It is too wonderful a thing to remain esoteric and too profound to be trivialized . . . For Teresa and John, the dark night of the soul is a totally loving, healing and liberating process. Whether it feels that way is another question entirely.'[2]

St John of the Cross knew this darkness personally and he came to love it. His life was marked by real darkness. Not long after John was born his father died. He, his mother and two brothers were forced onto the streets, becoming transients who moved from place to place in search of work. His mother eventually found space for John in an institute for disadvantaged children where he lived till he found work as 'a nurse-cum-porter' in a hospice for people dying from syphilis. At twenty-one, he left the hospice and joined a community of friars, where he trained to be ordained as a priest. Many years later, innocently caught in political battles within the order, he was arrested, imprisoned and subjected to emotional and physical abuse. He was imprisoned in an old unused toilet cistern in what he described as 'hour upon hour of interminable blindness'. The only light he had was a midday ray that poked through a slit, high in the wall of the prison, which served only to mock him as it passed on, leaving him in twenty-three more hours of blackness.

St John of the Cross experienced not only this physical suffering and darkness, but also inner darkness as he felt God withdraw and leave him in his despair. It is from these experiences that John writes of the dark night of the soul.

While John uses the imagery of the dark night, Scripture speaks of the desert. Both darkness and desert describe a foreign, previously unknown, inhospitable and obscure pathway. In both, we are stripped of the successes, achievements and learning of the past. In both, the very things we have learnt to rely on become useless. It is not simply church and the externals of faith that are wrong; something is deeply wrong in us. The ways of prayer that have held such richness often become vacuous and empty. People experiencing this chrysalis of the soul often talk of being bored when reading the Bible. They simply can't get into it. Scripture begins to bore us, irritate us or mock us as we seem so, so alienated from the God it describes. Eugene Peterson touches the essence of what is needed at this time in his translation of Matthew 11:

> Are you tired? Worn out? Burned out on religion? Come to me. Get away with me and you'll recover your life. I'll show you how to take a real rest. Walk with me and work with me – watch how I do it. Learn the unforced rhythms of grace. I won't lay anything heavy or ill-fitting on you. Keep company with me and you'll learn to live freely and lightly.[3]

Chrysalis time provides new space. It provides space for old ways to be set down and for new ones to emerge. It is the sort of space where growth occurs and change happens. This new space is like the belly of the great fish in which Jonah finds himself, or the desert experience of Moses and, later, the people of Israel. Sharon Parks describes this space as 'being shipwrecked', because in this space our faith comes apart and all that has served as a shelter and protection and has held and carried us, collapses around us. The structure that once promised trustworthiness is now dashed on the rocks. It is the space where we find we have no control: the space in which we are powerless. It is the space where we do not want to be, and from which we naturally want to run. We may want to run back towards what we have just left, or run recklessly onwards – running simply to get away from our present discomfort.

To describe this fundamental shift in our faith experience we have intentionally employed four images: the experience of the caterpillar entering the chrysalis, the dark night, the desert and being shipwrecked. These are all quite different images that arouse different understandings. Their difference is important because each one of our journeys is unique and different. Because of this, we need multiple metaphors to encourage us that there is hope and new life beyond, but also to remind us that our faith journey will be personal; we cannot follow someone else's path or fight other people's monsters. We must walk our own path, wrestle our own demons and live our own journey. The old French text of *The Quest of the Holy Grail* says that if the hero (heroine) 'wants to succeed, he must enter the forest "at a point that he, himself, had chosen, where it was darkest and there was no path"'.[4]

Whether we are propelled by suffering and difficulty, or drawn by new challenge and opportunity, we find ourselves in this still space. What is common in each of the images we have drawn on is the pain, loss and grief we experience as we enter this new phase of faith. This new space demands grief work: a time of letting go. It is a time to actually let go and, metaphorically, hang upside down like the caterpillar and wait – trusting that God will begin something new.

This chrysalis-like space is a space some have described as liminal.[5] Liminal space signifies an in-between area, a no man's land or a neutral zone. It is a space that is ambiguous yet sacred: a space that is the threshold of the new. Either suffering drives us, or adventure lures us, into this threshold space – this dark night which obscures all sense of the way forward; this desert that strips us of our past strengths; this crucible that holds us in the flame of God's presence; this chrysalis of metamorphosis. In this space we are invited to make friends with strangers and to face the monsters that threaten to propel us into self-destruction. While we may have met these strangers and monsters before, we now meet them face to face and are invited to make the strangers our friends and to ride our monsters down.

Strangers become friends

The strangers we befriend in this critical phase of our faith journey are like the wise men of Bethlehem; they come bearing gifts. The first of these strangers is darkness itself. While, no doubt, there have been previous dark times in our lives, this is quite different. This is the darkest of nights: deep and seemingly unending. We cannot see where we are going. We do not know what lies ahead. We cannot locate God or assess what God is doing in our lives or in the world. The darkness invites us to a new depth of trust in God and to an acceptance of our own vulnerability and lack of insight.

For St John of the Cross, the 'dark night is not primarily *something*, an impersonal darkness like a difficult situation or distressful psychological condition, but *someone*, a presence leaving an indelible imprint on the human spirit and consequently on one's entire life.'[6] John was forced to face this darkness and it became his friend. John tells us that the darkness is real. 'That is John's greatest gift: not so much to tell us what to do nor to pinpoint our place on the map, but to draw back the curtains and disclose the whole journey as real.'[7] In this critical passage, we too can no longer pretend that our own darkness does not exist, or that it is not real. Quite naturally and unashamedly, none of us enters the darkness easily. We all fight the darkness and this is normal; it is even encouraged by God. When periods of darkness come on us, we all long for the time before the darkness appeared. We all instinctively want to go back to when it was easier, clearer and less painful. Yet, sooner or later, we realize we must face the darkness and, in so doing, we begin to accept it. We are in the dark now. We do not have to lessen or fight or minimize our darkness in order for the light of God to shine. For the light of Christ is seen in the darkness. The Gospel of John introduces us to the God who enters the world by saying that Christ comes as light into the darkness of the world. 'The light shines in the darkness, and the darkness has never put it out.'[8] God as light is not only to be found if we can escape this darkness or get rid of this darkness; rather the light shines in the darkness.

Claiming that this light – Christ – enters the darkness does not underestimate for one second the depth and power of the darkness. What is being claimed is that the light comes in the despair and darkness. Whatever the specific darkness may be in our own individual lives, this passage reminds us that God comes as light in our darkness and God's light will never be put out by the darkness.

The second stranger is inertia. In the chrysalis, the busy active life of the caterpillar is stilled. Cocooned in the chrysalis, there is no room for doing; there is no opportunity for activity. This is the time of hibernation and of learning to simply be. This is the time where 'doing' must cease in favour of learning to 'be in the now' and of realizing our simply 'being' delights God. We don't have to do anything – God delights in us.

The third stranger is loss. Before we can move on, there will be much loss. There will be the loss of old ways of living faith; there will be the loss of our prized images and understandings of God, and there will be the loss of our sense of self-identity and role. With these losses comes grief: grief for the loss of a surety and a security of faith. There is grief for the loss of certainties as the black and whites of faith, ethics, theology and conviction open up to a wide expanse of unknown and unknowable greys. Painful memories can haunt us: memories of a time now lost. This is hard, emotional work, but it is also necessary. We must open up space to let the new come. I wonder if this is what Jesus meant when he spoke of the need to pass through the eye of the needle. In order to pass through, much baggage must be set down and left behind. We can't get through the eye with all this extra stuff. We will, as Mike Riddell's opening quote suggests, be stripped to the core before this is over. Yet these losses create the space in our lives for God to meet us in new ways.

The strangers of darkness, inertia, and loss confront us in our chrysalis of faith and though, at first, we want to ignore them and hide from them, we find that it is in befriending these strangers that new growth is achieved – they can become formational friends. But the darkness brings with it not only strangers, it also raises monsters. These monsters beckon us towards self-destruction; they need to be faced and acknowledged and, in Parker Palmer's terms, 'ridden down'.

Riding our monsters down

Parker Palmer[9] highlights five common monsters of the dark that many find they must ride downwards to the point where they see the power of these monsters in their lives and can truly acknowledge the power they have over them. Although there are five equally significant monsters mentioned by Palmer, I intend focusing in detail on the first, namely, the insecurity and self-worth that seeks to validate itself by external successes, possessions and confirmations.

I mention this monster first because it is has been so significant for me. I have been driven by external successes. Ironically, it has been in facing and owning failure that I have been given new freedom. An important part of my own dark night story has been coming to accept my failure as the site of my deepest experience of God.

The account of the prodigal son and Rembrandt's painting of the scene as the father and son embrace has been particularly helpful to me. We have a print of the painting hanging on our dining room wall. It is a painting that I return to often because I am constantly struck by the overwhelming, even foolish, love of the father. A copy of this painting also hangs in the meditation room of a Benedictine monastery that I have been to for retreats. I remember spending time reflecting on this painting at the monastery and finding myself drawn to the kneeling younger son. I had previously focused on the older brother and the father. But this time, perhaps for the first time, I was drawn down onto my knees like the younger son, with robe and hat removed, and shoes kicked off. Here, it was as if I was held in the embrace of the father. I was sensing his warmth, his tender touch and his loving gaze.

I think I had generally identified with the older son because of his attempts to do what is right, and to be responsible and reliable. However, on this occasion, I found myself drawn to the younger son, to his failure and to the father's identification and embrace of him in that failure. After reflecting on the painting for a while, I needed some exercise and so decided to go for a walk. The track I took led me down through wet and slippery grass into a beautiful valley. I was the only person for miles and the beauty of the valley on that winter afternoon seemed a personal gift. Was it given simply for me to enjoy? A small lake was below me; the willows dangled their leaves into the water's edge. The water was dead calm and mirror still. The pink and mauve of the willow seeds covered the edges of the lake as the golden light of the late afternoon sun passed through the branches and dark grey rain clouds rolled in across the distant hills. As I walked towards the lake, I was startled by a wood pigeon which was sitting on a branch right in front of me. It was very big and very close. We seemed equally surprised to find ourselves staring into each other's eyes. The wood pigeon's red eyes and green, grey and blue feathers were clearly visible. We watched each other for what seemed a long time, but was probably only a few seconds; neither of us dared to move. Then, as I gently edged closer, the pigeon stirred and flew away. I had frightened it; I hadn't meant to.

As I stood there, watching where the pigeon had been, I sensed something deep within me asking whether I meant to hurt the bird. 'Of course not,' I mentally answered the unanswered question. It seemed that the deep reply was, 'You are like this wood pigeon. Every time I try to get close, you run away – frightened. I won't hurt you.'

I carried on walking down the hill towards the edge of the small lake that I had seen when I first entered the valley. I was hoping to reach a seat that I could see on the far side of the lake. From that vantage point I would be able to watch the family of ducks that were gliding peacefully on the surface of the lake. But yet again, before I could reach the seat, the birds stirred and flew off. So I sat on the seat and looked at the lake where the ducks had been and thought about the ways in which I acted like a frightened bird that didn't let God get close.

Of course, at one level it was a very simple and easily explained couple of events. Some birds had flown away as they saw me approaching. There is nothing unusual in that. But for me, the desire to just enjoy watching them was destroyed as they flew away, frightened by my presence. Coupled with this was the small question deep within that suggested I am like them: frightened and flighty whenever the Spirit tries to draw close to me.

The walk with the birds by the lake and a gentle knock on my door that evening led me to read Henri Nouwen's book *Life of the Beloved*. I had planned to do a number of things that week while away on retreat, but they were now all set aside in favour of a slow reading of Nouwen's story. One of the monks had dropped it in for me, suggesting I might like to read it.

Nouwen's writing went straight to the core of my concern when he wrote:

> I am putting this so directly and so simply, because though the experience of being the beloved has never been completely absent from my life, I never claimed it as my core truth. I kept running around it in large or small circles, always looking for someone or something able to convince me of my belovedness … From the moment we claim the truth of being the beloved, we are faced with the call to become who we are. Becoming the beloved is the great spiritual journey we have to make.[10]

Nouwen went on, encouraging the reader to keep moving towards the truth of our belovedness by unmasking false feelings and reminding us of the truth about ourselves. 'The truth, even though I cannot feel it right now, is that I am the chosen child of God, precious in God's eyes, called the beloved from all eternity, and held safe in an everlasting embrace.'[11] He encouraged us to spend half an hour a day in this love – 'If you develop the discipline of spending one half-hour a day listening to the voice of love you will gradually discover that something is happening of which you were not even conscious.'[12] He encouraged us to celebrate this truth and to be thankful for it, saying, 'When we keep claiming the light, we will find ourselves becoming more and more radiant.'[13] But Nouwen's advice came with a warning: 'Not claiming your blessedness will lead you quickly to the land of the cursed. There is little or no neutral territory between the land of the blessed and the land of the cursed. You have to choose where it is that you want to live.'[14]

I'm not sure any learning has been as significant or so long in coming as this was for me: accepting that I am loved by God and that God delights in me, my resting, my relaxing, my relationships and, yes, even my work. For many years (even decades), I saw God as interested in my work; God was interested in what I could contribute, what I could give and what I sacrificed. While I believed in a free, non-works based salvation, deep within I saw God as chiefly interested in what I did and how I contributed to church, to mission, to people and to the world's needs. I sensed God's pleasure and knew it wouldn't matter if I did nothing at all from now on. God still held me. I have read endless books, sermons and papers on the acceptance of God and have written eighteen years worth of messages, many on the same theme, but none had brought me as deeply into that experience of being held. It was indescribable, yet palpable. The experience I had tried so hard to stay away from – deep failure – had become the site of a much deeper connection with God and of a new sense of freedom given by God. The stone the builder rejected had become the cornerstone.

The second common monster that Parker Palmer identifies is the belief that the universe is a battleground and hostile to our interests. This monster encourages us to believe that life is a battle and there are inevitable winners and losers. The world is full of scarcity rather than the abundant provision of God. Again Nouwen was helpful: 'To be chosen as the beloved of God is something radically different. Instead of excluding others, it includes others. Instead of rejecting others as less valuable, it accepts others in their own uniqueness. It is not a competitive, but a compassionate choice.'[15]

The third monster, functional atheism, afflicts people like me all too easily. Palmer describes what he means by 'functional atheism' as 'the belief that ultimate responsibility for everything rests with us. This is the unconscious, unexamined conviction that if anything decent is going to happen here, we are the ones who must make it happen.'[16] This, too, is a large part of my psyche and, I would suggest, a besetting monster for many in church leadership.

Palmer's fourth monster is fear. Here he points to our natural fear of the 'chaos of life'. We are deeply devoted to eliminating chaos and 'we want to organize and orchestrate things so thoroughly that messiness will never bubble up around us and threaten to overwhelm us'.[17] Rather than attempting to plan and control our lives and faith to protect ourselves from chaos, we need to leave room for it; we even need to invite chaos, for it is out of chaos that the Spirit creates. This time of chaos is necessary. In the open space of chaos there is the possibility of something new. Without chaos, nothing new can come. The open space is created and protected by honest grief work.

The final monster that Palmer encourages us to ride is our denial of death itself. What could be more fundamental in our culture than death aversion? The denial and sanitizing of death has become endemic. I am constantly surprised how families and friends want to fit the death of someone they loved into their schedule. A quick and professional funeral is what so many want. 'Don't drag it out; don't allow too much emotion.' 'Yes, it is sad, but let's not dwell there; we all have lives, appointments and other things to be moving on to.'

But it is not just human death we try to deny. There is also our refusal to allow organizations, programmes and societal structures to die. As Palmer states, 'Projects and programs that should have been unplugged long ago are kept on life support to accommodate the insecurities of a leader who does not want anything to die on his or her watch. Within a denial of death lurks another fear – the fear of failure . . . failure is always a little death.'[18]

The five monsters mentioned here are common examples of the false foundations and truths we need to uproot and destroy in the 'letting go' process of our own dark night of the soul. As we enter these times we need, Palmer suggests, 'To ride certain monsters all the way down, explore the shadows they create, and experience the transformation that can come as we "get into" our own spiritual lives.'[19] Our example in doing this is Jesus who understood the importance of riding his own monsters down. In the desert, he rode his own monsters as he was tempted to be efficient (turning stones into bread to overcome his hunger), to be powerful (having power over the nations of the earth) and to be spectacular (being able to jump off the temple and not be hurt or killed). Jesus went on to teach his friends that unless a seed falls into the ground and die, it will not produce anything.

Easter is our model. Easter is our account of God entering our darkness and journeying downwards. It is a journey, like our own, into an undefined and unknown desert space characterized by darkness and suffering. It is a desert of meaning; it is a darkness that hides all ways forward and a suffering that strips even God's soul bare. Easter, the greatest parable enacted by the greatest teller of parables, tells us that the crucifying power of evil, the burying power of death and the transforming power of love have collided.[20] They tell us that in the end the transforming power of love wins. Easter is our reminder that 'alleluia' is only heard through the agony and absence of cross and tomb, because God was prepared to enter the darkness.

How did God do this? First, God became human and, as an ordinary man, God chose not to act out of power and divinity, but from vulnerability and through hopelessness. It was something God had to do. The Gospels proclaim this necessity: The Son of Man must suffer many things and be rejected and be killed.[21] This journey was necessary. Guided by the Spirit, Jesus moved from his desert temptations to his final breath in full surrender of himself: both surrender onto the cross and surrender into the mystery of God. His dark night began in the agony of the garden where he could only anticipate what lay ahead. Here we are told that his soul began to be greatly distressed and troubled as he waited alone; his friends were asleep and his enemies were approaching. No one was there to support him as his anguished prayers that God would take this impending suffering away from him turned to the pure prayer of total surrender.

Then Jesus is kicked backwards and forwards by the religious and governing authorities. He is passed, unwanted, from the religious elite in the Sanhedrin to the Roman governor, to the Jewish king, Herod, and back again to Pilate who quickly passes him on to the angry mob. He is betrayed, abandoned, rejected and cursed, as the full force of evil overwhelms him. Jesus is left only to cry, 'My God, my God, why have you deserted me?'[22]

But this is only the beginning of his journey downwards. His next descent is into hell itself[23] – into the depths of God-forsakenness beyond all human hope. Jesus goes down into the deepest and furthest area of alienation from God and God's creation. This is the place of deepest silence. Here love between Father and Son is stretched to extremis. Jesus descends to be dead among the dead; he is alone with those irretrievably isolated and separated with those utterly alienated. As he descends to the utter bottom, as it were, the compassion of God is stretched to include these places and all he finds in them. Then Christ begins to rise in new hope, bringing with him a new vision where 'God will be all in all'. The love between Father and Son that had been stretched to the utter extreme is now drawing him up like a deep-sea diver's guide rope.

Here is the ultimate parable of what the dark night is all about. Though our experience will never embrace the fullness of Christ's, we are challenged to enter into and live our own dark night, with Christ as both model and guide.

Our own dark night will be unique. What is important is that we live it. That is the important step: the step that takes us into our own personal and unique dark night of faith. Henri Nouwen so clearly states the importance of this saying, 'It is better to feel your wounds deeply than to understand them . . . we cannot cover the hurts of our hearts with the bandages of the mind.'[24] So, we too, are invited to descend, as it were, into our own journey of faith. We are invited to descend into our own darkness, our own desert and our own suffering. This is our chrysalis of faith, where one form of faithful living must die and from this death, a new form is given life. This is the transformation and metamorphosis offered in the journey of the chrysalis. It is a transformation shaped by the strangers we invite to be friends and the monsters we choose to ride down.

Before a caterpillar can take shape and emerge as a butterfly, it must become at home in the darkness, the stillness and the seeming death of the chrysalis. The metamorphosis of the chrysalis, like the seed planted in the ground, is a process of both death and new life. The time of the chrysalis is tomb time: the time of cocooning before the miracle of new form. What is happening is a biological miracle. Yet it is all in secret, obscured from those who would like to watch. Quietly and unheralded, a miracle is occurring. Enzymes are being released that will digest all the caterpillar tissue, converting it into a rich ooze. Literally, the chrysalis becomes a bag of rich fluid. Inside this chrysalis, small cells, called 'imaginal disks', begin the process of metamorphosis as the ooze becomes wings, legs, thorax, abdomen and brain. Deep within the chrysalis, all the organs are being formed and connected together to form the intricate and minutely detailed structure of an adult butterfly.

We, too, will be marked by this chrysalis time, just as Jacob was marked by fighting with the Angel of the Lord.[25] From that moment on he walked with a limp and his name was changed to Israel: 'a man who wrestles with God'. This phase will transform us as radically as Jacob become Israel or the caterpillar turned butterfly. As the chrysalis closes around us, feelings of emptiness, loneliness, shock, anger and, probably, denial that we are even here take root.

Pierre Teilhard de Chardin prayed, 'O God, grant that I may understand that it is you (provided only my faith is strong enough) who are painfully parting the fibres of my being in order to penetrate to the very marrow of my substance and bear me away with Yourself.'[26]

This is hard emotional work. It is work that requires much energy, honesty and vulnerability. Yet, through this hard emotional work, ground can be cleared for us to encounter the Spirit in new, fresh and deeper ways. As Parker Palmer says:

My own experience with anguish has been that facing it and living through it is the way to healing. But I cannot do that on my own. I need someone to keep me standing in it, to assure me that there is peace beyond the anguish, life beyond death, and love beyond fear. But I know now, at least, that attempting to avoid, repress, or escape the pain is like cutting off a limb that could be healed with proper attention.[27]

In the midst of this difficult emotional work, when our own prayers so often seem empty, the prayers, like this one from the New Zealand Anglican prayer book, from those who have gone before often give courage:

Lord,
it is night.

The night is for stillness.
    Let us be still in the presence of God.

It is night after a long day.
        What has been done has been done;
    what has not been done has not been done;
        let it be.

The night is dark.
    Let our fears of the darkness of the world and of
        our own lives
    rest in you.

The night is quiet.
    Let the quietness of your peace enfold us,
        all dear to us,
        and all who have no peace.

The night heralds the dawn.
    Let us look expectantly to a new day,
        new joys,
        new possibilities.

In your name we pray,
Amen.[28]

The truth is we have no idea how long the night will last. For some people, the night doesn't come to an end. It lingers and enfolds us and is driven often by depression, grief, confusion, doubt and despair. For others, the darkness, like the desert, is sought because the person feels positively drawn to move deeper and deeper into it. For many, the darkness is experienced for a time while deeper transformations are underway. However long the darkness lasts we know we are with God. God is at work in the darkness, for the light shines in the darkness and the darkness will not overcome it.

5

From Deep Within – *letting come*

The chrysalis becomes home

The chrysalis provides a sturdy cocoon in which the caterpillar is protected from the outside world and given uninterrupted time for transformation; yet the space within must be large enough to allow the butterfly to take shape without being limited or constricted in such a way as to permanently damage it. Providing just enough space is a careful balance as the chrysalis needs to be both protective and spacious.

So, too, individuals in the crucible of faith change need space and time. They need time and private space for the new self to tiptoe to the surface. The chrysalis stage of faith is an intensely private and internal phase because what is emerging is initially fragile and vulnerable. It is a phase that we naturally don't want to advertise. Something new and deeply personal is taking place as we slowly find a sense of who our God is and how our God relates to us. We therefore need a spacious space, a protective space and a space that keeps us connected to the heart of Christian faith.

I have used a rope illustration to explain this balance to people in churches. Holding the rope, I have suggested that people exploring and re-forming their Christian faith need to know that we, their church community, are holding one end of the rope as they hold the other. This means that we are holding to faith in Christ, prayer, Scripture, Christian community and so on. But they also need us to give them a lot of rope to explore and find their own way. That is, we are not trying to keep them on a short leash. Both are important. It is important for each of us to know that the chord of faith we hold on to is anchored firmly by others and to know that we are being given freedom to explore and find our own way. If there is too much rope, a person is cut free to drift and wander without a centre or anchor. If there is not enough rope, they are stifled from exploring their own way forward with God. This is the same tension required by the chrysalis, which must remain both attached to the host plant and also distinct from it.

Chrysalis time is an important time when the grace and the acceptance of God can impact us profoundly. It is a time when we come to know that we are loved by the God-of-all-that-is. We are warmly welcomed by this God as we are and who we are. The chrysalis time is, for some, an experience like the prodigal son's. Remember Luke's description of the father running in abandon to meet his son. Remember the warmth of the father's embrace. Remember the way the father disregards his mentally rehearsed speech, preferring to hold his bedraggled and pig-smelling son close to his chest. Remember the ring that the father takes from his own finger. This ring signifies his power, authority and status. Remember the party he throws and the pride he shows, as he celebrates his homecoming – to the startled amazement of his neighbours and friends. For many, the chrysalis time is a time when the acceptance and delight of God for them personally is encountered afresh: encountered deeply. For most of the people I have talked to, it is a slow incremental awakening to the fact I am accepted. The God-of-all delights in me.

Bacon for breakfast

Imagine the prodigal son waking up the morning after coming home: the morning after the party. After months, maybe years, of living the hard life, he wakes up in a comfortable clean bed and a quiet room. His first thought must be that he has been dreaming. The father's response and the party must have been a dream. But then he feels the ring on his finger: a tangible reminder that this was no illusion. From here I am extrapolating the story well beyond Luke's records. He gets up and goes out to find dad cooking breakfast and the smell of bacon.

Why bacon? Luke clearly tells us that the father's response of love for the son breaks all the rules. He runs to meet him, when he should be more dignified. He embraces him, when he should chastise him. He disregards the son's prepared speech, as he hugs him to his chest. He takes off his ring, the symbol of his identity and authority, and gives it to him. In so doing, he reinstates him as his son and heir, to the horror of those looking on. Instead of showing his anger at the boy for running off and being reckless, he throws a party. Instead of showing his disappointment at his son's unrighteous and sinful living, the father joins in the partying. Instead of caring for his own pride and position in front of his family, neighbours and friends, he foolishly and lavishly shows his love and compassion for him. The father's attitude seems to be, who cares if they see my tears and my unbridled delight? My son is home. It is the way in which the father breaks all the rules that allows me to enjoy the idea that he cooks bacon for breakfast.

Pigs were seen as unclean. Any Jew who worked with pigs or ate pig meat was also seen as unclean: someone to stay away from. But the father doesn't stay away. He breaks the rules for the sake of love. The father has watched and longed for him and in the process he has found the most important thing of all – his love for him. Now, he is not afraid to display that. His running, his embrace, his ring and the party all show this change in the father. The bacon simply carries the rule-breaking of the father through into the next day. It suggests that this is a permanent change, not an isolated event in the father-son relationship.

The father, who represented authority and the rules of right and wrong, has changed to the father whose natural response is love. The relationship between father and son has changed: changed for ever. This graceful encounter is somehow richer because of all the time spent with the pigs.

That time created a hunger and longing for both father and son. St Augustine of Hippo said somewhere that yearning made the heart deep. It also makes you vulnerable.

Graceful encounter

The crucial learning of the chrysalis is that our God becomes a God whose dominant face towards us is one of generosity and compassion: a God who is far more interested in delighting in us as a friend than worrying about what we do. In experiencing this new welcome and acceptance we are invited to relate to our God as friend rather than master or CEO. While God remains God, God's primary face to us has changed. As this happens, the chrysalis becomes a precious crucible of change. It becomes a place of gold.

Jesus talked of this shift in relationship as he prepared the disciples for his imminent trial and death when he said, 'I no longer call you servants, because a servant does not know his master's business. Instead, I have called you friends . . .'[1]

This is the core encounter with God in the dark night. It is the encounter of grace and friendship in which we are accepted, embraced and delighted in simply for who we are. The Bible talks about this grace in many different ways as justification, redemption, reconciliation and so on; in essence, whatever term or metaphor is used, they all mean we are deeply and painfully loved. We are accepted and we belong in the universe of God's creation and community. In the chrysalis, this love is tested and found to be true. We are not loved as we would like to be. Our God is no benign Santa that simply does what we want. Our God is the God of all time and space who reaches into our lives with a care, acceptance and invitation that only God can give.

To illustrate this core encounter of the dark night we will draw on the account of theologian Paul Tillich, lyrics from a U2 song and the description of the pastor and political activist Dietrich Bonhoeffer.

Paul Tillich describes this encounter, saying:

Grace strikes us when we are in great pain and restlessness. It strikes us when we walk through the dark valley of a meaningless and empty life. It strikes us when our disgust for our own being, our indifference, our weakness, our hostility, and our lack of direction and composure has become intolerable to us. It strikes us when, year after year, the longed-for-protection of life does not appear, when the old compulsions reign within us as they have for decades ... sometimes at that moment a wave of light breaks into the darkness, and it is as though a voice were saying: 'You are accepted. You are accepted by that which is greater than you ... simply accept that you are accepted! If that happens, we experience grace. After such an experience we may not be better than before, and we may not believe more than before. But everything is transformed ... and nothing is demanded of this experience, no religious or moral or intellectual presupposition, nothing but acceptance.[2]

When U2 brought out the album *All that You can't Leave Behind*, many of their lyrics conveyed the sense of being encountered by this acceptance and grace. Perhaps the clearest of these is found in the song 'Grace' which describes how grace carries our pain and shame. Including how God's grace overcomes barriers and dissolves antipathy; making ugly aspects of our lives and past sites of pain into places where God's new life may be encountered.

Yet this is no cheap grace. It is not costless acceptance. Perhaps no one has explained what costly grace is better than Dietrich Bonhoeffer when he wrote:

Costly grace is the treasure hidden in the field; for the sake of it a man will gladly go and sell all that he has. It is the pearl of great price to buy which the merchant will sell all his goods. It is the kingly rule of Christ, for whose sake a man will pluck out the eye which causes him to stumble, it is the call of Jesus Christ at which the disciple leaves his nets and follows Him.

Costly grace is the gospel which must be *sought* again and again, the gift which must be *asked* for, the door at which a man must *knock*.

Such grace is *costly* because it calls us to follow, and it is *grace* because it calls us to follow *Jesus Christ*. It is costly because it costs a man his life, and it is grace because it gives a man the only true life. It is costly because it condemns sin, and grace because it justifies the sinner. Above all, it is *costly* because it cost God the life of His Son: 'you were bought with a price,' and what has cost God much cannot be cheap for us. Above all, it is *grace* because God did not reckon His Son too dear a price to pay for our life, but delivered Him up for us. Costly grace is the Incarnation of God ... costly grace confronts us as a gracious call to follow Jesus, it comes as a word of forgiveness to the broken spirit and the contrite heart. Grace is costly because it compels a man to submit to the yoke of Christ and follow Him; it is grace because Jesus says: 'My yoke is easy and my burden is light.'[3]

In trying to give words to this graceful encounter and explain the inexplicable we have over-simplified. How do we give words to a personal encounter with mystery? How do we give words to an encounter that is at once so real and transformative and yet so utterly personal and unique? Karen Armstrong draws on a poem by T.S. Eliot in her attempt to explain her own journey and then ends by saying, 'And yet, of course, it wasn't like that at all. I am trying to describe an experience that has nothing whatever to do with words or ideas and is not amenable to the logic of grammar and neat sentences that put things into an order that makes sense. Maybe I could explain it better if I were a poet.'[4] St Teresa's explanation only sounds even more confusing: 'The will must be completely occupied in loving, but it does not understand how it loves. The understanding, if it does understand, does not understand how it understands. Or at least it cannot comprehend anything of what it understands. It doesn't seem to me that it does understand, because, as I say, it does not understand itself. Nor can I understand this myself!'[5]

As inexplicable and palpably undeniable as an encounter with the grace of God may be, in and of itself, this is not the end. For in the context of love's acceptance, love challenges us to become. In the silence, the question is asked, 'What are you going to do with the rest of your life?' I imagine the prodigal father asking this question of his son as they eat their bacon breakfast together. I imagine the conversation going something like the conversation between the resurrected Jesus and Peter as they ate breakfast together on the beach. John's Gospel describes Jesus asking Peter if he truly loves him and if he is willing to serve him. After all that has happened, Peter knows his own frailty and failures, but he is still able to answer 'Yes'. Often, in the face of that question, we too are aware of the smallness of what we can contribute and perhaps of previous failures. But juxtaposed beside this, we are aware that we are powerful. We can act, and act meaningfully. In that mix of our own smallness and insignificance and yet our ability to act meaningfully, we are asked to look ahead: to look ahead in wonder and imagination. We are asked to explore our deepest desires and ask, 'I wonder if I could?' When such wonder and imagination meet, vision is born. Such a vision can frame our thinking and our actions as we begin to consciously move into it.

The inexplicable transformation of the chrysalis

What actually happens in the chrysalis? 'Inside, far from curious eyes, an incredible process takes place. The caterpillar quite literally dissolves into a sort of primal ooze, a real mess. And then, following directions coded somewhere in that mess, the raw protoplasm reaggregates, and what was once a crawling beastie now has the hardware to fly.'[6] In effect, the caterpillar goes to its essence (its spirit) and then re-forms, or better, transforms, into a totally new way of being. There is no way of getting from caterpillar to butterfly except by passing through the void.[7]

The transformation has been hard work. While it seemed that nothing was happening, a great deal of energy was being expended. During the chrysalis phase nearly half the weight of the adult caterpillar was lost. The process of metamorphosis has consumed a tremendous amount of energy. Before the butterfly emerges, the chrysalis becomes transparent, allowing the sun's rays to penetrate. Being cold-blooded, Monarch butterflies often need this external warmth to invigorate them. Maybe we are similar. Before we have the energy to emerge, we too may need to bask in the Son's warmth. For we too cannot underestimate the demanding emotional and spiritual work completed in the chrysalis of the soul. This soul work that has been done has drained us.

Then there comes a time to leave the chrysalis. The internal yearning of the Spirit that led to us leaving the busy, activity-focused faith to hibernate and go inward now draws us back towards others again. The chrysalis has been for a period of time; it held us in transition and transformation, but it is not for ever. Now it is time to emerge.

6

Being Alongside – *accompanying*

To be Christian is to be communal. Lone ranger Christianity is an oxymoron. The Christian faith was never meant to be lived alone. How can we live as lone rangers when we follow a Trinitarian God who at every point models and invites us into relationship? Our need for connection, if not our desire for it, is greatest as we traverse the dark nights of faith. The research we have carried out with people in crises of faith and church involvement indicates that this phase, the phase of the dark night, is the one phase in the journey of faith where people most need to be connected to a group, or a spiritual director, or close friends. While they need to be given space to move away from old ways of 'doing faith' and given the freedom to explore their own new ways, they also need to be accompanied. Our longitudinal research, which tracked people over a five-year period, shows the significant influence of being connected to faith groups, churches, spiritual directors and supportive friends. With few exceptions, our research showed that those people who moved into a clearer, stronger and more definitive Christian faith had been accompanied in their journey.[1]

Again, we can learn from the caterpillar. When the caterpillar has shed its last skin, it forms a strong connection between the chrysalis and the silk anchor point. From here the chrysalis will hang until the butterfly is ready to emerge. It is a vitally important connection. The chrysalis needs to be held while the metamorphosis within the chrysalis takes place. If the chrysalis drops to the ground, or is laid on its side, it will inevitably lead to the malformation of the butterfly. People moving through a significant faith transformation are similar. Although there is a strong tendency to move away and isolate ourselves from others, we also need some connection with the wider community of faith. Our connection may only be to one person, maybe a spiritual director, or to a small group of others, who can understand and empathize with us. But we do need to be connected to someone who can accompany us through the dark night of transformation. Without such accompaniment our chrysalis can become our grave. If we are left alone in this chaotic time, there is too great a risk that our faith will slowly die.

Jesus invited others to accompany him. He modelled letting others in. He allowed others to see his deepest vulnerabilities and struggles. He did not hide his scars and wounds but 'let Mary wash them, Thomas touch them and his mother hold them. What vulnerability and courage! I want to hide my wounds; I want to protect them, and not let anyone see. Jesus, on the other hand, openly cursed, openly wept and openly blessed. He modelled a transparent life and carried his cross through the streets.'[2] Painful though it is, we too need to be openly and honestly connected to at least one other person of faith through this transformation time. Whom we choose to accompany us is a very important choice.

St John of the Cross is very clear that some advisors are simply 'blind guides'. They don't know what they are doing. Because they have not walked their own dark night paths and explored beyond the pre-critical phases of Christian faith they cannot advise, understand or support someone else. Ironically, many Christian leaders and ministers fit into this category. In times of faith crisis, what we need is someone who can validate our journey, who can help to normalize it for us and offer the hope of a deeper Christian faith beyond the chaos we find ourselves in right now. This is scary stuff and we need to be accompanied by someone who can be a sounding board that reflects back faithfully, hopefully and with love. This accompanying role is a very significant one: one that can take a number of forms.

Small groups

Over the last eight years we have developed a network of
small groups[3] that people who are struggling with faith and
church concerns could be part of. The groups have been
informal and have provided space for people to explore their
faith in an open-ended way. They have included: people who
had been abused by controlling church cultures; people who
wanted to explore faith questions without being told answers;
people with life experiences that caused profound doubt of
God; people who were hurt, angry or bored with Christian
faith, and people hungry for spiritual reality. The groups have
provided a space where people with new ideas and thinking
and with questions and doubts of any kind could openly
explore them. They have given a space where people could
say anything and where nothing was considered heretical.
They have provided an open space, in which no one was
considered a guru and where there was room for everyone
to contribute to and shape the conversation. Each time these
groups met, certain guidelines were established to protect the
space:

- We are not trying to produce one answer that everyone
  must adhere to.
- There is freedom for differing views and opinions and
  we ask for respect for those, no matter how different or
  heretical they might sound.
- We ask for respect and space for each person who comes
  and for their opinions.
- We cannot 'fix it' for people who come.
- Because this is a conversation, we ask that each person
  speaks relatively briefly.
- We have no neat 'tie-up' at the end.
- We let God defend God.

For people willing to do the hard emotional and spiritual
work involved in faith transformations, these groups were a
tremendous support and encouragement. Typically, individuals
would be part of the group for around eighteen months. This

approximate time frame seemed to give people the space they needed to deconstruct and then reconstruct their faith. Once the reconstruction work was done, individuals' need for the groups tended to wane. Most then moved off to other communities, groups, contexts or churches that better suited their new phase of faith.

Spiritual direction

Faith crises and transformations are bread and butter work for spiritual directors. The accompaniment of a good spiritual director through crises of faith is simply invaluable. They are, I believe, the greatest resource available to us in faith crises, for we can share our own story with our director, receive affirmation and validation for our journey and be given specific books, prayers, poems, pictures and concepts to take us further. Perhaps, most of all, spiritual directors draw us back to seeing where God is with us and where God is inviting us into new experiences and understandings.

Wise friends

For many, spiritual direction and groups like those described above are not readily available, but wise friends are. If we turn to friends to accompany us, we need to ensure they are both wise and strong friends. Wisdom within faith transitions means a willingness to let us tell our stories, share our hurts, express our doubts, rage and rave against God without becoming defensive or withholding the hope of the Spirit of God at work with us. They need to be people who are comfortable with mystery and paradox and able to draw on many styles of prayer and who have searched for God deeply. But they also need to be strong friends: people who are willing to walk with us knowing it could be a long and bumpy journey. In an article on the deserts of faith, Doug Reichel included a letter from a friend who exhibited this wise friendship and concern. He says:

After walking out of our church I knew that my withdrawal would also be from a close friend for a season. We had met weekly for four years over breakfast to talk, banter ideas, sharpen and pray for each other. But I could not talk or banter or sharpen or pray any more, so I wrote him a long letter explaining. He wrote back a card that accompanied a particular wine we had enjoyed together. That card and bottle became for me a moving symbol of all that friendship could be in the darkest hours. It was fleeting, like the scent of roses unexpectedly pushed past your nostrils by a wind gust – but I smelled hope. In the card were written the following words:

I respect your need to be silent, to withdraw for awhile – I'll be silent with you. Thanks for letting me know why. Please know that I trust you and our friendship. It's hard to be distant, to walk afar off, but we'll weather this new dimension to our friendship. I'm crying silently with you. Please accept this bottle of Pinot Auxerrois as a token of my trust in you and our friendship – and the hug that comes with it.[4]

Unexpected companions

If a chrysalis becomes disconnected from the stem or leaf, it can sometimes successfully be glued back on. An artificial connection can be made between the chrysalis and the plant that will continue to suspend the chrysalis while the critical transformations occur within. Ironically, unexpected companions can do the same for those in the midst of faith crises. When we look at the desert and dark night experiences of the biblical characters, we see that God sometimes sent the most unusual people to accompany them. Melchizedek came to Abram in his desert wanderings and Jethro, the Midianite priest, came to the assistance of Moses. Both of these companions knew the desert and were messengers from God. Yet they stood outside of the group from which Abram or Moses might have expected help to come. Melchizedek is an eerie character who simply appears in the narrative as if out of nowhere and disappears in the same way after he has met with Abram. We know very little about this character who the biblical record says has no genealogy, no father or mother.

All we know is that he was the priest who introduced God's people to the symbolic meal of bread and wine. The word priest literally means 'bridge'. A priest is therefore someone who bridges the divide between humanity and God. This is what Melchizedek does for Abram and he is recorded in the book of Hebrews as such. He is a prototype of Jesus, the great High Priest.

In our own dark nights of our faith we should not be surprised if unusual priestly figures (those who bridge the divide between ourselves and God) draw alongside. They are a gift from God, for they help to beckon our true self into being, and they help ground us while a new faith identity emerges.

Whoever our companion or companions are through this critical passage of faith, the most significant support they can offer is to listen.. Until we are heard, we cannot hear! We need to be heard; we need to be *really* heard before we are in a position where we can hear anything others might want to say. The most helpful thing a companion can do is to stand by us with a genuine commitment to try and understand our position and our feelings.

We should not underestimate the power of such listening as a helpful, even healing, role in people's faith journeys. When such listening is non-judgemental and accepting, it provides the context in which pains, abuses, questions, confusion, doubts and heartaches can be verbalized and, most importantly, heard.

Our research and experience in accompanying people suggests that people want to be heard, but they want to be heard in particular ways. What are the qualities of such listening?

Non-judgemental listening

It is crucially important that the listening be non-judgemental. The majority of people struggling with church and faith have significant questions or hurts about church, the Bible, prayer and God; they need to talk about these. The listening they require is non-defensive. They need the kind of listening that does not try to defend the church, or the Bible, or even defend God. People need to be encouraged to verbalize what they feel and believe. If they are angry, let them talk about their anger. If they are hurt, let them describe that hurt and what it has done to them. If they have questions and doubts, let them put those 'out there', so that they themselves, and others around them, can see them objectively.

Face-value listening

Each person's story has to be taken at face value. At times, people will make comments about church leaders or Bible passages or failed prayer that appear 'over the top', exaggerated, only half the story, or simply untrue. At such times, the kind of listening that is required is a listening that accepts that this is truth as it is experienced by this person right now. It is their truth and, whether or not others might agree, it is the truth they are acting out of. It is true in its consequences. Face-value listening accepts a person's perspective. It does not attempt to question, change or add to their perspective but, rather, lets it stand.

Provisional listening

The corollary to face-value listening is provisional listening. Provisional listening means accepting that this is the person's viewpoint, feelings or understanding at this point in time. They may well change with time, and probably will.

Listening for the unsaid

It is essential to the art of listening that we carefully watch body language and notice emotions as well as arguments, and pauses as well as words. When we probe an emotion, point out a bodily reaction, or name a feeling, this can often open up new understanding and depths of communication.

Skilled listening

A skilled listener knows when to seek professional support and when to refer a person to a counsellor, medical doctor or to someone more theologically trained. For example, the dark night experiences of faith are often confused with depression. In fact, they often co-exist. A skilled listener is aware of the signs and symptoms of depression[5] and can advise a potentially depressed person to seek medical support. A person's faith journey is not helped in any way by being depressed and it is always important to seek medical support if we suspect signs of depression. As Gerald May says, 'There is a persisting notion in some circles that the medications used to treat depression and other psychiatric illnesses can somehow interfere with deeper spiritual processes such as the dark night. Nothing could be further from the truth. To my mind, there is never an authentic spiritual reason to let any illness go untreated.'[6]

Long-term listening

People's faith questions are not resolved quickly, their pain is not healed instantly and their confusion does not clear in a night. Therefore, the kind of listening that is required is long-term. It is both hugely daunting and positive for the listener to realize this. It is daunting because it reminds us that to really be a companion for this person, a substantial amount of time is required. It is reassuring because it reminds us that no matter how dark, angry or confused the person may be when we meet them and no matter how inadequate our responses may be, one conversation will never be 'the answer'; it will need the long journey of many conversations.

Painful listening

The listener must really hear the pain of the other person. In this sense their role is simply to absorb some of the person's pain. Their role is not to minimize it but sympathetically and, if possible, empathetically, to share in their pain and confusion. This is the kind of listening that hears the cry of the other person, takes on something of their pain and offers that pain in prayer to God.

Incarnational listening

As people raise their doubts, anxieties, past hurts and abuses, it is often helpful if they can be listened to by someone who represents, at least to some degree, the church, the faith, and even the God whom they are questioning, railing against and attacking. For this reason, I sense it is very important for those who listen to be committed people of Christian faith. Ministers, pastors, church leaders and spiritual directors can play a unique role as key listeners.

This kind of listening can be summed up as 'loving listening'. It is the kind of listening that leaves room for and anticipates the graceful encounter between the person accompanied and the Spirit. Those who listen and accompany are beckoning the inner authority and identity of the individual to the forefront. This is not the time for telling them, or instructing them, or worse still, acting for them. The support they need at this time is the accompaniment of people who are themselves immersed in the deeper stories, promises, metaphors and values of the Christian faith. They need people who do not so much give advice as give images and metaphors that help a person reframe and re-evaluate their own faith. Finally, those who accompany need to be future-oriented, making available the hope of a future that does not exist as yet.

7

Going Solo – *emergence*

Emergence from the chrysalis is a delicate business for the butterfly. So too is emerging into a new self-constructed and self-owned faith. For both faith-journeyer and butterfly, it can be a tentative and demanding step: a step that is full of risk. It is a step we must make on our own. In faith terms, it is the step to re-emerge into a community of faith, to move towards making our own contribution, and towards living more fully our vocation with others and the world. There is much risk in such steps, but our own growth depends on taking them. If we try and stay in the chrysalis for ever it becomes our grave. Much courage is needed now. There are no short cuts. There are no easy, ten-step recipes.

Emerging from the chrysalis of faith is not easy. The foreign and lonely place of our faith chrysalis has become home. This phase of our faith has provided a new internal wellspring for our faith and logically we want to stay there. Telling others of our faith seems risky. Rejoining a community of faith seems risky. Following deep hints that we could give ourselves to others in particular ways seems risky. But a risk only really becomes a risk if we take it. And this is what the time of emergence from the chrysalis into a post-critical faith invites us to do. Some aspects of the faith journey have to be traversed alone. This will be a time when we may feel vulnerable in front of others and misunderstood. Our emergence will demand every ounce of strength and perseverance we have, but without moving beyond the chrysalis we don't develop the strength of faith and character needed for the next phase.

An apocryphal story suggests that a little boy came upon a butterfly struggling to emerge from a chrysalis. He helped it to emerge by gently pulling the chrysalis apart. When the butterfly tried to fly, it fell to the ground and died. The strength it needed to develop to emerge from the chrysalis was the same strength it needed to fly. The boy tried to help but inadvertently made the butterfly helpless. The story ends suggesting that sometimes we need to struggle to build up our strength to grow and develop so that we can cope with what life will throw at us.

This is a threshold time. Do I have the courage and determination to step over this threshold into a new way of living out my faith? At this time we may draw inspiration and courage from the emerging awareness of the disciples that Christ had risen and was inviting them to follow him in new ways.

When the resurrected Jesus appears, his new life is only slowly experienced, realized and understood by those who were close to him. When Jesus appears to them, they are at their most down and depressed moment. They are disillusioned, experiencing grief and feeling a sense of shame. Feelings of failure and betrayal pervade their conversations. So their awareness and appreciation of the risen Christ is slow to dawn. While Jesus stands directly in front of them and speaks to them, eats with them, and even lets them touch him, their despair and hopelessness slowly thaws. It takes time for a dawning sense of the new reality to grab them and begin to transform their understanding. This event is like a black hole in the experience of the disciples. The ordinary laws and expectations of their religious perceptions are being changed irreconcilably. They stumble to appreciate that love, God's transforming love, is free to appear on its own terms and to inspire its own hope. They cannot predict or manufacture it; nor can they, or will they, deny it. This is the revelation of ultimate love that changes the very sense of the universe. A tomb that had been sealed by darkness and death is now opened and emitting a light and love that they struggle to appreciate. In the darkest of their nights new glory shines.

Our emergence from our own transformative experience of faith may be like the dawning awareness of the disciples as Jesus appears to them beyond death. Often our own emergence from a dark night experience can have much in common with the disciples' adoption of a post-Easter faith.

When a friend contemplates emergence from their faith chrysalis, the only help they require is someone to accompany them. The timing, approach and work of this threshold moment will be theirs alone. As the story of the little boy and butterfly reminds us, no one can do the emergent work but the butterfly. Nevertheless, a passive supporter is often a great encouragement.

The process of emerging from a faith transformation involves at least two significant steps. The first is the step to re-engage in a community of faith. The second is to begin to contribute to others and the world based on our own unique sense of personal vision, vocation, calling or contribution.

Re-engaging into communities of faith

Having withdrawn into the chrysalis time of faith and gained so much personally from a protracted time away from the often frenetic activities of church, there comes a time when we sense it is 'right', 'possible' and 'necessary' to re-engage. To continue to develop our own faith, we realize that we need to connect with, learn from and contribute to others. Such re-engagement means becoming involved with and contributing to a Christian community, not simply visiting a church now and again. It involves taking the step to find a church, a small group, or a faith context in which we can share our faith with others again. It is especially important to connect with people who are at different phases in their own journey of faith. We need to hear their stories and be encouraged by their passion and commitment, and also bring our stories of the chrysalis journey of faith to encourage and support others. This is the step towards communion: a common unity with others in Christian faith.

Finding our vocation

The second step is the step towards generativity, towards
giving of ourselves to others. This is where our fragile sense
of our own vocation begins to take shape. Fredrick Buechner
defines vocation as 'the place where your deep gladness
meets the world's deep need'.[1] Parker Palmer points to the
beginning of this quote:

> Buechner's definition starts with the self and moves toward
> the needs of the world: it begins, wisely, where vocation begins
> – not in what the world needs (which is everything), but in
> the nature of the human self, in what brings the self joy, the
> deep joy of knowing that we are here on earth to be the gifts
> that God created.[2] … Vocation does not come from a voice 'out
> there' calling me to become something I am not. It comes from
> a voice 'in here' calling me to be the person I was born to be,
> to fulfil the original selfhood given me at birth by God. It is a
> strange gift this birthright gift of self.[3]

This is the rebuilding and reconstruction phase of chrysalis
time. It is the time when we sense a new way of living: a
way of living which is congruent with our deepest sense of
ourselves and what we desire to do and be in the world.
Again, finding our sense of vocation is a painstaking task.
No part of chrysalis time is easy. This is the place for deep
and difficult emotional and spiritual work. Palmer puts it
like this:

> The soul speaks its truth only under quiet, inviting, and
> trustworthy conditions. The soul is like a wild animal – tough,
> resilient, savvy, self-sufficient, and yet exceedingly shy. If we
> want to see a wild animal, the last thing we should do is go
> crashing through the woods, shouting for the creature to come
> out. But if we are willing to walk quietly into the woods and sit
> silently for an hour or two at the base of the tree, the creature
> we are waiting for may well emerge, and out of the corner of
> the eye we will catch a glimpse of the precious wildness we
> seek.[4]

I read these words of Palmer's sitting in a park overlooking Sydney harbour. We were en route to Europe and had some time to kill in Sydney. It was a hot day: too hot for sitting without some shade. But the thought of the twenty-four hours or more cooped up in economy class that lay ahead of us encouraged us to enjoy the sun and stretch out. After a while, it just got too hot and I was becoming increasingly uncomfortable. On a deeper level, I sensed how so much of what I was doing, and the expectations I was striving to reach, were undercutting my own vocational imperative from being given space. The two feelings were colliding. A sense of being trapped in too many expectations and, therefore, of being unable to really pursue my sense of my vocational imperative (this is what I need to do) was linked to an entrapment on the park bench in the direct summer sun. Thinking that the only way out of the sun's heat was to abandon the seat and move onto the rough ground nearer the shade, I suddenly realized that the park bench was not concreted into the ground. In fact, I could easily, so very easily, move it under the shade of the nearby tree. As I did this, I became aware of just how much freedom I had to restructure my priorities and living patterns to better fit my sense of vocation. It was that simple. I could move things and thereby stop being trapped. Of course, seeing what I could do and then choosing to do it, with all the risks that entailed, are two different things. What was important for now was that I had a vision of a way forward.

At this point it was a very fragile vision. Sharon Parks explains this sense of fragility: 'Fragile here is not intended to connote weak, feeble, or puny. Rather, it is more like the fragility of a young plant as it emerges from the soil – healthy, vital, and full of promise, yet vulnerable. The feelings are those of special promise, hope, glimmering possibility, challenge, and sometimes exhilaration . . . there is also risk of disappointment, failure, exclusion, abandonment, emptiness and hopelessness.'[5]

The hints we received in the chrysalis space of who we could be and of what we have to give to others, or what we need to do now, begin to take shape as we emerge into contexts where we can contribute to others. I say begin to take shape because we have to trial and prototype our sense of what we are to do. We have to reflect on the impact of living in this way for ourselves and others. As we live in new ways, we have to ask certain questions. 'Is there a sense of the Spirit with us?' 'Do others sense the Spirit in what we do?' 'Do they sense freedom, beauty, compassion, order etc.?' Through this slow process of praxis (action followed by reflection and evaluation and then more informed action) there can be a crystallization of our sense of the way forward.

Crystallizing of intent

I am very reluctant to use the word vision as it carries so much societal and church baggage. It is a word that is overused and often misused. But it is also the right word to describe the compelling sense of being drawn into a new way of living. It is becoming who we were destined to be. It is our DNA taking shape in the way we live. It is our own imago cells that carry the designing information for our lives, beginning to frame our living. It is becoming who we are called to be.

I could speculate on how a butterfly must feel as it steps off the branch to try out its wings for the first time. It is a dangerous and courageous step. In our own transformations we too are called to emerge from our own chrysalis time in order to fly. A butterfly that walks around the edge of its chrysalis and around the plant on which it has always lived is not a butterfly. To be a butterfly, it must fly. So too must we.

We don't know if butterflies have thoughts like this or not. We don't know if they reflect on what is happening to them but, the fact is, we do. As we let the Spirit of God open new ways to us in the darkness of our own chrysalis of faith, a vision emerges of being who we are called to be. Now it is time to give life to those visions. It is time to move beyond just dreaming about our vision; it is time to let go of the chrysalis and fly. What a scary thought!

Parker Palmer says, 'In our time we have forgotten the ancient wisdom that the self will wither if we seek it directly, and will flower only as we lose it in service of others.'[6] This is a reminder that personal fulfilment is gained through being generative and that personal growth is established through self-giving, not self-seeking.

Paralyzing vision

It was in the darkness that our vision took shape as wonder and imagination combined to sketch the possible. But such a vision can also be paralyzing because we feel that for our vision to be a real vision, it needs to be big. Yet our sense of what we are to do may feel quite small. We often carry a sense that to truly live our destiny we need to do something that will change the world. This simply is not true. What we sense in the darkness comes to life in how we live and what we do, not in the size of its influence. Mother Teresa is quoted as saying, 'You cannot do great things. You can only do small things with great love.'

At the point of emerging we need to focus on how we do what we sense we are called to do, rather than focus on the impact of what we are called to do. Our obedience to ourselves is to live who we are and to do so in ways that express the grace and love we experienced in darkness.

Our vision can also be paralyzing because so often we don't know how to bring it to life. The only way forward is to hold our sense of vision lightly, knowing that it will both strengthen and evolve. What we have now is a tentative idea that needs to be tried. So, the important thing to do is to just try it. Imagine the butterfly again. It will never fly if it wants to have it all planned and wants to know all about flight before letting go of the chrysalis and trying to fly. The butterfly learns to fly by flying. The same is true for our own sense of emerging vision. We learn to become who we

are called to become by doing it. Of course this will seem
awkward, unusual and tiring at first. But the more we do it,
the more our innate nature and the Spirit will guide us. It
becomes increasingly natural. As we live the way we were
designed to live, we thrive. This is what we were meant to
do. What initially seemed awkward very quickly becomes
graceful. We can become an *'instrumentum conjunctum cum
deo':* an instrument shaped to the contours of the hand of
God. This is the ultimate purpose of the transformative faith
journey.

'Instrumentum conjunctum cum deo' describes a wonderful
place in the Christian life. It is the place where we become
willing and useful instruments in the purposes of God. We
become instruments that God has fashioned and prepared for
personal use. St Ignatius knew that God wants to shape us and
make us ready for the Spirit to use as favoured instruments:
instruments that fit perfectly in the hand and purpose
of God. Father Thomas Green[7] illustrates *'instrumentum
conjunctum cum deo'* by considering the favoured knife of
the butcher, the knitting needles of the knitter, and the pen
of the writer. In each case, a particular 'tool' that has been
used again and again becomes the favoured choice of the
worker because it fits so neatly in the worker's hand. Over
time it has been moulded and shaped to better fit the user's
hand. And whether we think of the knife of the butcher, the
knitting needle of the knitter, or the pen of the writer, we
realize these tools of choice are often not the most attractive
or expensive of the instruments available to the worker
– but they are his or her first choice and the most trusted.
The dark nights of faith, if we yield ourselves to them,
ultimately shape us to be the *'instrumentum conjunctum cum
deo'* of the Lord Almighty: instruments that God can use. We
become instruments that through constant wear and usage
become a perfect fit for the hand of God. This is not always,
or probably ever, an easy process as rough edges are worn
smooth. Yet, surely, it is better to be the instrument of choice
in the Master's hand than remain in a pristine and unused
state in a plastic wrapper. Subtly, our focus shifts from what
we may personally learn or gain to what God is doing with

us for God's own purposes. This is what it means to be generative and, ironically, in this phase of Christian faith it is in being generative that we sense the Spirit in our lives and continue to mature in awareness of God. This is because we are increasingly aware that we are being formed and shaped through life to be willing instruments in the hand of God. And in the end, while we are being shaped to better fit God's purposes, we have birthed within our very selves and souls new depths of hope, faith and love.[8]

A story is told of St Francis of Assisi:

> As he and a friend, Brother Leo, entered the centre of a village, they saw a man leaning against a stone wall playing a small wooden flute. The music he played was sweet and melodic and Francis began to dance happily in the street. Within minutes a crowd gathered to watch the strange but interesting way he swayed to the music, back and forth, leaping in the air with his arms outstretched. Brother Leo was embarrassed but the man playing the flute and the crowd that had gathered greatly appreciated his dance. When Francis stopped dancing, everyone in the crowd, which had by then grown to over fifty, began to applaud wildly. Even the man leaning against the stone wall showed his gratitude and clapped his huge hands together. Though Francis was nearly out of breath, he launched into one of the impromptu sermons he was famous for … 'Oh, Lord, make me an instrument of your peace,' he prayed … 'carve me into a flute that is placed to your Divine lips, and fill me with the breath of your spirit. Wrap your fingers around my soul and cover the holes of my life. Make of me a song to the Beloved ….'
> Later, Francis explained to Brother Leo the meaning of the two key words 'instrument' and 'your' from his now famous prayer 'Lord, make me an instrument of your peace' saying, 'Each of us is called to be an instrument of peace. And yet it is only when we surrender to the Divine current within that we are played, just like the flute. Otherwise we are as silent as a reed, anticipating sound and music, imagining the flow of wisdom and insight that leads us nowhere. Until we realize the futility of trying to play ourselves, we are like an instrument that sits in the corner of the room. It is soon forgotten by everyone in the house … it is the tomb that brings us to life, Brother Leo, not death. It is like the tomb of our Lord who saw the futility

of death, then rose to eternity. Likewise, we too will experience the futility of our ego and rise to a life that exists beyond our hollow definition.'[9]

8

Imago – *being*

Beyond the chrysalis, the Monarch butterfly flies. When the butterfly flies we see the beauty, the fineness and the fullness that the caterpillar always promised, but could never really exhibit. The adult caterpillar, now fully transformed, flies aerodynamically and gracefully with beautifully coloured wings.

Biologically speaking, the Latin name for the adult stage of development is imago. Here, in the adult butterfly stage, the imago shows through. The caterpillar has become what it was intended to be. Similarly in our journeys of faith, after the transformations of the desert we become increasingly the people we were intended to be. Our image, the imago given to us by God, begins to shine through. We become who we were called to become. This is the phase of being in which living our faith is far less about what we do and far more an expression of selfhood. The selfhood that was formed in the silent, dark months of chrysalis now comes to life. The work of this new phase is to live increasingly in this selfhood. It is the invitation to live our gift that becomes our work beyond the chrysalis. What was formed in darkness, seclusion and privacy is now to be offered to the light, to others and to our world. This is the invitation to the butterfly. It is the invitation to fly: to move towards the place where they will mate and lay eggs. In reality, it is a destination that is often tens, hundreds, even thousands, of miles away.

The invitation to each one of us beyond our own chrysalis of transformation is to live the gift God has given us. It is the invitation to live the gift breathed within us in the chrysalis of faith. It is the invitation to let our new life, energy and vision be seen, be risked and be offered to others.

This is a demanding and stretching invitation. It is an invitation I have observed many people moving into. One springs to mind immediately. She is a woman in her fifties who had a very successful career and business as an independent midwife. This was a profession she had enjoyed for more than twenty years. Yet in the radical transformation of her faith, a new dream began to emerge: a dream of caring for the dying. It was a dream that emerged as she completed a long period of personal retreat and spiritual direction. To follow this dream was a risky move, professionally and personally. It would mean leaving a known and successful career, a good income and a profitable business to start at the bottom as a nurse and carer of people in a hospice. She hadn't been a general nurse for years and had never worked in a hospice situation. It meant lower pay, much lower status, less career certainty and some unpleasant work. She would be the one to change beds, wash patients and tidy up faeces, urine, vomit and blood. Perhaps more significantly, she would move from the excitement of new life to the grief and pain of imminent death. And yet the dream to care with a realistic, practical love for those who were dying had been planted within her. I spoke to her recently and heard some of her stories from the hospice; it made me aware of just how much of a lived gift she is becoming.

Of course, the gift we are invited to live may not involve a change of work role or work at all. It is about being who we are. It is about living our gift and this may be expressed equally in our family, community or present work context. The contexts are less important than following the invitation to be and to live the dream: to begin living the vision of new life that we experienced in the transformation of the chrysalis. Often, the invitation of a new way of being is not even a new invitation. It may be something that has been pulsating inside us for a long time. It may be a dream that has lain latent in our being, or a dream that we have followed and are now invited to enter more fully and completely with no compromises.

Living our truth

Sharon Parks describes watching a film with a group of university students about the life and work of the famous psychiatrist, Carl Jung. In the film the interviewer asked Jung, 'Do you believe in God?' Jung immediately responded, 'No.' At this response, many of the students who were watching laughed spontaneously, assuming, of course, that Jung was too sophisticated to believe in God. Jung, however, continued, saying, 'I don't have to believe in God, I know God.' 'This time,' Parks states, 'no one laughed.'[1]

Here, Jung is expressing a mature faith shot through with conviction. This is not the old 'certainties' of a previous, external, authority-bound faith, but an inner core of wisdom and conviction. 'Jung exemplified a strength of knowing that [*is aware that*][2] all knowledge is relative; he knew that what he knew on any given day could be radically altered by something he might learn the next day. Yet he embodied a deep conviction of truth – the sort of knowing that we recognize as wisdom.'[3]

This same wisdom is exemplified in the response of Joan of Arc at her trial. It is a mature wisdom of faith that does not escape from, but rather engages with, complexity and mystery.

At seventeen years of age Joan of Arc was her country's heroine. Barely two years later she was executed as a heretic. In fact, she was burnt alive after a sham of a trial that was politically motivated against her.[4]

One account of her trial suggests that when the prosecuting bishop said the voices she followed were evil, she replied:

> That is your belief, Bishop, but not mine. Each must believe for himself. Each soul chooses for itself. No other can choose for it. In all the world there is no authority for anyone save his own soul. And, if I give my life for that choice, I know this too now. Every man gives his life for what he believes. Every woman gives her life for what she believes. Sometimes people believe in little or nothing, nevertheless they give up their lives to that little or nothing. One life is all we have, and we live it as we believe in living it, and then it's gone. But to surrender what

you are and live without belief – that's more terrible than dying – more terrible than dying young.

The prosecutor, warning her of the penalty for heresy, then said, 'Before it is too late, do you know what that means, Joan? It means the fire.'

Joan replied, 'To live your life without faith is more terrible than the fire. And if it were to do over, I would do it again. I would follow my faith even to the fire.'

And to the fire she went; she was burnt at the stake at nineteen years of age. It takes courage and strength to live our truth with the conviction and grace shown by Carl Jung and Joan of Arc. This maturity of Christian living can be both strong and graceful because, in the chrysalis, it has encountered the wounding love of God and it is marked for ever by such grace.

Living in our own skin

An old Hasidic tale about the importance of living my own life, fulfilling my own vocation, and walking my own path is told by Rabbi Zusya. He said, 'In the coming world, they will not ask me, "Why were you not Moses?" They will ask me, "Why were you not Zusya?"'[5] This is the invitation to live our own vocation, knowing we are not called to be someone else but to be fully and completely ourselves.

Historic Christian understanding had a word to describe this new unique selfhood: they called it our *charism*. In the writings of St Paul, the term *charism* has a double meaning. In the broad sense it designates the 'gift' of Christian life in general, while in the more strict sense it meant a particular or specific 'gift'. Hence, a *charism* is a living gift; it is a breath of the creator Spirit within individuals or groups.

Someone I spoke to recently described this new phase as being able to live fully within her skin, realizing both how powerless she was in the bigness of the world's needs, but also how powerful she was. There is a lot in this sentence which needs unpacking. First, she was living fully within her own skin. By this she meant that she was expressing herself fully; her *charism* was her life and it was being lived fully. She was not holding back, masking or depreciating who she was any more. Living this way brought her in touch with her own powerlessness and the smallness of the influence she could have in a world of such huge need. And yet, at the same time, she was aware that her very small influence was nevertheless very powerful.

As this woman said, 'I am small and insignificant but I can do my bit and my bit matters. It is big and powerful when I fully live my own reality.' Somehow, the journey through our own chrysalis of faith, and our emergence from it, encourages us to see the paradox of our own gifts and energy. Of course we are small and insignificant. We can't change the world and are unlikely to become *Time* magazine 'person of the year' but, nevertheless, we are paradoxically very powerful. We are influential. We are significant. How we live out our faith is powerful but, like the butterfly, often not in a way we can see, predict or control. The flap of the butterfly's wings may be linked to a tornado on the other side of the world, but the butterfly in flight doesn't anticipate that and cannot be aware of it.

Living in our skin is owning what we can't not do and doing it. As Parker Palmer put it, 'This is something I can't not do, for reasons I'm unable to explain to anyone else and don't fully understand myself but that are nonetheless compelling.'[6] It is living our life, despite the fragility and vulnerability we feel.

Imagine for a moment the thoughts of the butterfly (assuming of course that they think as we do). All through its life the butterfly has crawled around the leaves of one or two plants. It has dragged itself slowly and heavily around in search of new food. It has never travelled very far or very fast. Then, while immersed in the chrysalis, the vision to fly has come. We might call it instinct, or call it vocation, or call it DNA. Whatever we call this vision, it is a vision to do something that the butterfly has never done before.

Living graciously and gracefully

James Fowler describes the journey of faith as being like a dance. It is a useful metaphor. I am not a dancer. At six foot four and with the co-ordination to match, dancing is not something I find easy; I was put in a remedial marching class when I joined the military. My wife and my daughter, on the other hand, are both dancers. To them it is natural. They have a feel for the rhythm and they move easily to the music. As dancers, they are graceful. This is what living our vision is like. It is like being a graceful dancer that moves to the call and rhythm of their own internal music. Post-chrysalis, one could truly call the dance of faith, graceful.

The most significant marker of a post-critical faith is its graciousness. I am watching a butterfly in flight as I write. It moves gently and easily as it flies, riding small wind currents and gently alighting on a leaf before moving on again. It is so graceful and natural to watch. Watching a butterfly flying gives hints of how post-critical, faithful living is natural; it is almost instinctive and integrated with the life of the person.

While each person's chrysalis time is unique and intimately personal, each desert experience and dark night of soul are characterized by one universal characteristic. This is the experience of being touched by grace: that undeserved and unearned acceptance and love of God. In our personal wilderness experiences, such grace is no longer simply understood conceptually, but becomes intensely and personally experienced. At the darkest moment in our dark night, we realize we are held; we belong, and we are accepted. It is something that must be personally experienced in order to be lived out. No theoretical or conceptual knowledge will compete with this profoundly core experience that 'I belong'.

Through much of our Christian journey we gain only a relatively shallow understanding of God's grace. Somehow, only the surface is touched as we conceptually and intellectually come to understand that God loves us. Like the caterpillar with its tough outer skin, the knowledge of God's love doesn't really get into the core of how we see ourselves and affect the most intimate parts of our self-identity. But in the chrysalis, when everything is reduced down to a primal ooze of core beliefs and personal life experiences, a profound sense of acceptance, forgiveness, being held and being loved can permeate us. This is the Spirit at work in our deepest and darkest places and it profoundly and irretrievably changes us.

Post-chrysalis people do many different things. They make many different kinds of contributions; they live very different lives and are involved in all manner of vocations, roles and contexts. But what characterizes them is the graciousness they show in what they do. To be gracious means to act mercifully or compassionately.

Drawing on the story of the prodigal father in Luke 15, Elisabeth Moltmann-Wendel describes the prodigal as realizing she is loved and deeply accepted by God.[7] In this crucial encounter, the prodigal learns that she is good, she is beautiful and she is whole. She says, 'God needs us as ones who have accepted themselves as good and whole [as God sees us][8] and thus enabled to renew through themselves the disturbed and destroyed creation. God needs us as ones who are beautiful and who can break through the vicious cycle of self-hate and contempt of others.'[9]

Richard Rohr sums up what it means to live in our own skin, to live our own truth and to live grace-fully saying:

> Mature Christians live by faith, not certainty. They become content within their own skin. They are calm, rounded human beings; they have a sense of themselves. Not that they are completely self contained; but they know what they don't know. They are attentive and present to the world as it is. You feel safe with such people; they don't threaten you, you don't fear them. They have a forgiving attitude towards reality. Violence is abhorrent to them. They are not fanatics or 'one issue' people.[10]

9

Butterfly Effect – *flying*

After emerging from the chrysalis, butterflies live quite differently from the way they lived as caterpillars. They no longer crawl with scores of little legs across their host plant; they fly. They are no longer eating machines that devour the green leaves of the swan plant; now they feed on the nectar of flowers. They no longer have a carefully camouflaged and tough outer skin to hide them from potential predators, but bright, colourful and eye-catching wings. The butterfly cannot act like a caterpillar or choose to go back to being a caterpillar, or even to the stillness of the chrysalis. An undeniable transformation has occurred and, because of it, everything has changed.

St Teresa reminds us that having emerged from the chrysalis of faith we need to live a post-critical faith. This means that our new ways of praying, worshipping, studying, serving and contributing have all changed through our chrysalis experience. We can no more go back to the old ways of prayer or any other aspect of Christian living than a butterfly can go back to being a caterpillar. In fact, trying to practise our faith as we used to is counter-productive. Perhaps this change is most poignantly felt in the need to find new ways of prayer.

Prayer

However we describe prayer, we come to recognize that beyond the chrysalis of our faith, our times of reflection, contemplation and stillness are vitally important to us.

Through them, we access the Spirit to live well. I liken this to the fact that butterflies are cold-blooded. Unless they are warmed by the sun, they are unable to maintain the energy they need to live. Monarch butterflies need the heat of the sun's rays. A few weeks ago a butterfly fell on our carpet floor and looked every bit as if it were dying. But after spending a few hours on a window sill flooded with the sunlight, the same butterfly flew away energetically as though nothing had happened. Living faithfully beyond dark night transformations in our faith depends on continual inner renewing through prayer. From now on, prayer cannot be faked for we depend on it for our very survival, as a butterfly depends on the sun.

Prayer that connects

In many ways butterflies are mysterious. We know butterflies communicate but, to date, we don't know how. Although they cannot hear, it seems that they do exchange information with each other. We know that butterflies will congregate in trees by their hundreds or even thousands, but we don't know how they arrange this. In a now famous experiment, twenty living Monarchs were placed in fine nylon bags and then hidden behind clusters of leaves hanging from the branches of trees. Within 20 minutes, free-flying migrant butterflies approached the trees; some rested on branches near the butterflies in the bags, while a few flew into the leaves to come to rest on the bags themselves. All the researchers could conclude is that Monarch butterflies do communicate in some manner as yet unknown.

The unidentified communication of butterflies reminds us that when we communicate in prayer we may not know what is happening, yet, nevertheless, we are connecting with a much bigger reality – the Spirit of God. As we learn to connect with the Spirit of God, we learn to act in concert with the Spirit. While our actions may be small and seem insignificant, when they connect with the work of the Spirit they are mysteriously influential.

The flight of the Monarch butterfly is graceful and fragile. Their wings are small and very fine; they can be so easily damaged. But we should not let their size or fragility lead us to underestimate their power. Butterflies can fly at speeds of up to 55 kilometres per hour and in their migrations they travel thousands of kilometres. Perhaps the best-documented migratory journey is from Washington to Angangueo in Mexico; it is a journey that takes a Monarch butterfly around two months to complete. Monarch butterflies are powerful little creatures.

But the true impact of the butterfly's flight is not measured by speed or distance covered, but in what we have come to call the butterfly effect. The butterfly effect tells us that when a butterfly flaps its wings the effect is potentially far greater and more wide-ranging than we might expect from simply watching the butterfly in flight. This butterfly effect is ascribed to Edward Lorenz who gave a paper in 1963 to the New York Academy of Sciences entitled 'Does the Flap of a Butterfly's Wings in Brazil set off a Tornado in Texas?' Lorenz was referring to an aspect of chaos theory, in which small variations of the initial conditions of a dynamic system may produce large variations in the long-term behaviour of the system.

The butterfly effect informs or reminds us of the interconnected nature of the lives we lead. The smallest of our actions at one point in time can have enormous repercussions down the track because they are connected. We do not see the connections or downstream influences of our actions and so we too readily trivialize the impact we have. The butterfly effect reminds us that our world's natural ecology is a complex interconnected system; so too is the world of human relationships.

Living faithfully is fundamentally different after we emerge from the faith-transforming dark night of the soul. There is a much greater awareness that we are deeply connected to God, to others and to the world around us. Gerald May sums up the essence of this change, saying, 'In my experience the most universal change accomplished by the passive night of the Spirit is the blurring of one's belief in being separate from God, from other people, and from the rest of creation. Increasingly, one feels a part of all things instead of apart from them.'[1] This is the Christian faith equivalent of the butterfly effect. With this deep sense of interconnectedness often comes a heartfelt longing for the kind of prayer, contemplation or reflection that strengthens our sense of connectedness.

Prayer that perceives

While prayer can take many forms, and any particular form chosen by an individual is almost irrelevant, the need to centre one's self and to connect deeply is an appetite that only seems to grow in the post-critical phase of faith. As this centring and connecting prayer develops, so too does another faculty that post-chrysalis faith and post-chrysalis butterflies share – the ability to perceive what was previously hidden.

Monarch butterflies are highly perceptive. In fact, they see the broadest visual spectrum of any known animal. They see colours and even UV light that we humans simply cannot see. We are unaware of much of the visual perceptivity of the Monarch butterfly.

A corresponding heightened perception and understanding is often gained through the darkness and pain of a transformative journey of faith. What the post-chrysalis people of faith perceive with much greater clarity is what motivates and lies behind people's actions. Having sat with their own suffering, their own pain, their own disappointment or disenchantment and, often, their own failure, post-chrysalis people are more profoundly aware of their own humanity. This heightened sense of their own humanity enables them to connect with the humanity of others. They are more able to sit with others in painful places. They are less frightened by the life experiences, grief or beliefs of others and they do not need to protect themselves or their faith as they might have needed to once. They are more comfortable to accompany and see the real needs of another, especially the need to be accepted and loved. In their common humanity, a link can be formed that transcends the barriers of behaviours and beliefs.

Christian faith before the journey through the dark night tends to be focused on the externals of people's lives – what they do, whom they associate with, what they say and how they behave. Judgements are important, and people are included and excluded on the basis of what they drink or don't drink, their sexual expression, what they wear, where they work and what they say. Post-chrysalis faith is able to perceive another layer that is most often closer to the core of a person. They are able to perceive a shared humanity.

Prayer to find our way

How do butterflies find their way? When they migrate, how do they know which way to fly? We don't know how they navigate – they just do it. Somehow, deep within lies a knowledge, or instinct, or compass that guides them.

Again, links can be made from the Monarch butterfly to living out Christian faith. In the mystery of all that happens through our own dark night periods of faith we are transformed. Often, part of this transformation is the mysterious gift of an inner compass – a gut feel for what we should do.

Maybe the story of St Brendan the Navigator can provide us a model and inspiration of what I mean by this inner authority and compass that develops for people. Brendan lived over fifteen hundred years ago, yet his life speaks to us across the centuries about the ways of navigation, both as a sailor and a man of Christian faith. Brendan's home was a mountain monastery, till he sensed a call to set sail for new lands to take the gospel. After fasting and praying for forty days, he stood on one of the beaches of southern Ireland and looked out across the ocean. In front of him lay a small boat. It was a simple boat, just leather skins smeared with animal fat stretched across a wooden frame. It was a flimsy craft for what would become, for Brendan and his companions, a seven-year journey from Ireland to Wales, Iona, Scotland, France, Iceland, Greenland and possibly even America.

The oldest account of St Brendan's explorations dates from the tenth century. Many of the details are debated. Historical fact and inspiring myth seem interlinked. Did he reach America? It is possible that he did. Some of his descriptions of the land he found indicate that he may have. But, if he did travel such large distances, how did he navigate? The common icon of St Brendan gives an interesting clue. In these iconic pictures, Brendan is depicted holding a paddle in one hand and a large Celtic cross in the other. Old burial sites indicate that Celtic crosses may have begun as a form of navigation aid: the first sextants. If so, it was the first sextant known to humankind.

Is this myth or historical fact? We will probably never know. But I am inspired by the notion of St Brendan navigating with a simple cross through the storms and times of being becalmed.

It takes real courage to set out trusting our own internal compass: the deep place where we have met God and the sense of who we are called to be that has emerged from within us. It is the same courage and commitment that Brendan must have needed as he followed the internal call of the Spirit to set sail into an unknown ocean and future.

Imagine the fearful-faith and courage he feels as he sets sail. A prayer attributed to Brendan opens a window on his feelings:

> Shall I abandon, O King of mysteries, the soft comforts of home?
> Shall I turn my back on the native land, and turn my face towards the sea?
> Shall I put myself wholly at Your mercy,
> Without silver, without a horse, without fame, without honor?
> Shall I throw myself wholly upon You, without sword and shield,
> Without food and drink,
> Without a bed to lie on?
> Shall I say farewell to my beautiful land, placing myself under Your yoke?

Shall I pour out my heart to You, confessing my manifold sins
And begging forgiveness, tears streaming down my cheeks?
Shall I leave the prints of my knees on the sandy beach,
A record of my final prayer in my native land?

Shall I then suffer every kind of wound that the sea can inflict?
Shall I take my tiny boat across the wide sparkling ocean?
O King of the Glorious Heaven,
Shall I go of my own choice upon the sea?
O Christ, will You help me on the wild waves?

10

Looking Back – *seeing the whole*

It is now time to reflect more deeply on the whole journey of faith development. I want to focus our attention on looking back and seeing the whole – this whole story of Christian faith transformation. As indicated in Chapter One, there are a number of ways to describe the transforming nature of Christian faith. But for many people, the heart of adult faith development is expressed in an invitation to move beyond pre-critical expressions of Christian faith, through a dark-night type experience, and into a post-critical faith. Of course, different theorists and writers have explained this in different ways. The French Philosopher Paul Ricoeur described it as the move from a naïveté of faith through a desert of criticism and into a second naïveté of faith.[1] Professor James Fowler speaks of a move from a conventional faith into a period of faith dislocation and self-focused exploration towards a paradoxical and mystical understanding of faith embraced with deep integrity. Briege O'Hare, an Irish contemplative, speaks of the transition from certainty to searching and on to intimacy.[2] Walter Brueggemann also describes a threefold movement in the prayers of the psalms from orientation to disorientation and on to reorientation. He says:

> The first naïveté is the precritical. It believes everything, indeed too much. It is an enjoyment of well-being, but unaware of oppression and incongruity. It is a glad reception of community, but unaware of hurt. It can afford to be uncritical because everything makes sense. But growth – and indeed life – means moving to criticism: a new awareness of self in conflict, of others

in dishonest interestedness, of God in enmity … But the second naïveté is postcritical, not precritical. The second naïveté has been through the pit and is now prepared to 'hope all things'.[3] But now hope is after the pit. It now knows that finally things have been reduced and need to be reduced no more. It knows that our experience is demystified as it must be. But it knows that even in a world demystified and reduced, grace intrudes and makes all things new.[4]

Put simply, and somewhat crudely, the primary metamorphosis of adult Christian faith is the move from a pre-critical faith through a period of hyper-critical faith towards a post-critical faith. The crucial part of this metamorphosis is what happens in the hyper-critical phase: the phase I have equated with the chrysalis transformation of the Monarch butterfly. Brueggemann calls this the journey through the 'pit'; Hagberg and Guelich call it the journey through the 'wall'.[5] St John of the Cross speaks of the 'dark night of the soul'; Sharon Parks speaks of the experience of being 'shipwrecked'. For Moses and the people of Israel, it is the 'desert experience'. However we describe this fundamental journey of faith, it is very real. It is very scary – and it is the critical journey in Christian faith.

Continuing with an oversimplification of this journey through darkness, I want to describe ten characteristics of the journey.

- It is the journey from faith understood in black and white, right and wrong, true and false dichotomies into the hyper-critical focus on the greys of life and faith. In this hyper-critical phase the black and whites are rejected in favour of a celebration of the greys of theology, morality and ethics. The move beyond hyper-critical faith to a post-critical faith involves the embracing of the black and whites and the greys with equal respect.
- It is a journey from dependence into a hyper-independence that shuns the influence of others, towards a growing interdependence that can be characterized by humility, vulnerability and deep connection.

- It is a journey from uncritical and tacit acceptance of answers into a mindset full of doubt, questions and critiques and on to an embracing of mystery, of paradox and a childlike delight and wonder.
- It is a journey from doing (being God's servant), into personal failure and acceptance of incapacity and on to a deep sense of God's delight and acceptance of who we are as God's friends. We are people who can simply be.
- It is a journey from living a role or roles into a period of self-identity formation and on to a new giving of self for others.
- It is a journey from trusting in, and being strengthened by, external authorities (e.g. church leaders, the Bible, etc.) into an internally based authority that is willing to be responsible for one's own faith, beliefs and life decisions and on to a growing acceptance and integration of both internal and external voices.
- It is a journey from an *effortful faith* to a *doubtful faith* and on to a *restful* and *thoughtful faith.*
- It is the journey from a faith like Martha's, which is troubled by many things and worried about all that has to be done, into a faith like Mary's, which is able to choose the one thing that is necessary, and on still further into a faith that expresses both Mary's heart and Martha's hands.
- It is a journey from a faith that needs mentors, leaders and disciplers to lean on, into a faith that is encouraged by those who sponsor and support the individual's own exploration and on into a faith that draws on others as co-discerners in the will and leading of God.
- It is a journey of faith from external truth, towards a growing trust in self-truth and on to an embracing of communal truth, symbolic truth and paradoxical truth.

Of course, what I have described with these ten characteristics is a gross generalization. But, as Gerald May summarizes, it is the essence of the writings of St Teresa and St John of the Cross:

Teresa and John both say that God deals with each soul with 'esteeming love' addressing each of us with profound respect for who we are and what we need and can bear. And though the process of this soul journey cannot be rigidly categorized into stepwise stages, it is a process, and it is going somewhere.[6]

This is not a journey that most Christians take. Most adult Christians are not invited, or thrust, into this fundamentally transformative journey. Sadly, many of those who begin the journey seem to get lost or sidetracked along the way. Of those who are invited, or driven, into the chrysalis of faith, too few emerge from the darkness into a stronger personal faith. Too many lose their faith, or retain only a shadow of their past faith that does little to motivate, sustain or shape their ongoing life.

The transitional changes from one phase to another can be very difficult for the person involved and it may seem, quite literally, as though their faith is being destroyed. This feeling can carry on for long periods of time: it can sometimes last for years, rather than months. It is because faith stage transitions are often so difficult, painful and protracted that people can get stuck in the midst of transition. As Professor James Fowler's faith stage theory illustrates, a move to a new stage of faith involves substantial core changes at every level of the way we understand and live our faith. He suggests that each stage of faith is marked by *change* in each of the following areas:

- The way the person thinks and understands their faith.
- The degree to which they are able to appreciate another person's point of view.
- The way they arrive at moral judgements and decisions.
- The way and extent to which they draw boundaries around their faith community.
- The way they relate to external 'authorities' and their truth-claims.
- The way they form their world view.
- The way they understand and respond to symbols and metaphors.[7]

It is because this journey is so demanding and fraught that I wanted to write this butterfly story. I wanted to provide something of a rough scaffold or a sketchy map that both normalizes what is happening for individuals and provides some hints of what may lie ahead of them. But also, most significantly, I wanted to offer hope in the midst of the journey's struggles. I wanted to offer hope for those in the midst of the journey that there is much gain from the passage through the chrysalis of faith. This is the kind of hope that God offers us through Isaiah and Deuteronomy:

> And I will give you the treasures of darkness and hidden riches of secret places, that you may know that it is I, the Lord, The God of Israel, Who calls you by name (Is. 45:3 Amp.).

> He [God] found him in a desert land, and in the howling waste of the wilderness; he encircled him, he cared for him, he kept him as the apple of his eye (Deut. 32:10 ESV).

11

Monarch Waystations – *being strategic*

When caterpillars metamorphose into butterflies, not only do they change, but their habitat has to change as well. As a caterpillar, they were dependent on one or two host plants. Their habitat was limited. The transformed butterfly is quite different. It doesn't eat leaves but nectar and it is not dependent on a few particular plants, or even one garden or geographical area. The butterfly is able to travel swiftly and easily from nectar source to nectar source.

The corresponding change of habitat for post-critical faith people is very difficult for people with a pre-critical faith – and especially their leaders – to understand. I have often heard the question, 'Why don't these people commit to a church in the same way they used to?' The answer is quite simply that what they need to nurture their faith has changed. The contexts they will draw from and give into have, typically, increased substantially and their sense of loyalty is globally, rather than singularly, located.

Post-critical people seem to flit as gently and move as easily as butterflies. They are no longer committed, grounded and dependent as they were before. For church leaders with a pre-critical faith this response lacks commitment and loyalty and can seem quite threatening.

This summer there has been a noticeable reduction in the number of Monarch butterflies seen in New Zealand. Newspaper articles and the television news have highlighted the loss of butterflies, but no clear reason has been found for their seeming decline. Interest groups have enouraged people to grow swan plants in their gardens to ensure there is an adequate number of host plants for Monarch butterflies to lay their eggs.

Throughout the United States, the planting of swan plants, nectar plants and other butterfly food sources is even more strategic. All along the migration path of the Monarch butterflies, from Mexico to Washington DC, people are being encouraged to grow plants that butterflies can feed off, because the migrating butterflies need plenty of regularly spaced food sources. Such strategic planting is necessary because, over recent decades, farming practices and extensive use of herbicides has greatly reduced the butterflies' food supplies. Added to this are the enormous increases of residential land, factories and housing developments that further reduce the natural food supplies. One source has suggested that up to three thousand acres a day was being converted from farm land to houses, factories, shopping centres and parking lots across the migratory paths. This insatiable appetite for development is seriously endangering habitats for Monarchs.

To overcome this problem and to allow sufficient food sources for the Monarchs a group called 'Monarch Watch'[1] are working towards the goal of over ten thousand patches of swan plants and nectar plants. They are calling these patches of Monarch habitat, 'Monarch waystations'. These are intermediate stations for the journey providing desperately needed food sources on the butterflies' migration routes. Without nectar plants the butterflies will not be able to migrate southward in the autumn, and without swan plants along the route north during spring and summer, they will not be able to lay eggs on food sources that allow the young caterpillars to grow. The call is for people to strategically plant resource-rich waystations.

Waystations is also a term I have used to describe churches and faith communities that foster and support faith development through the dark nights of the soul and on into robust post-critical forms of Christian faith.[2] Our research on people who leave churches ended by describing many church leavers as 'wayfarers': those who are exploring ways forward as Christians in a new context.[3] These 'wayfarers' need waystations. They need places where individual explorers can find and form communities that provide deep wells for finding truth, forming identity, encouraging spiritual desire and engaging a changing world. The relationship between wayfarers, *people* seeking to form a culturally relevant Christian faith, and waystations, *places* that foster, fund and develop such a faith, is hopefully obvious.

But what are faith waystations? I want to suggest they are spaces that allow individuals to take seriously their own faith stories and the stories of the Christian and biblical tradition in the context of their own lives and communities.

Waystations for Monarchs and Christian faith come in many different forms. Some are large, providing resources for many; others are smaller, catering for a few. Waystations of Christian faith can be churches which provide resources for those in significant faith transitions as a substantial part of their work. Waystations can also be smaller groups that support individuals, or the one-to-one spaces created by a spiritual director, pastor or friend, which were highlighted in Chapter Six. Added to these are the increasing array of waystations found in cyberspace in blogsite discussion forums and websites.

Whatever the form, the waystation provides a place or a space for an individual to explore and find meaning, develop identity and connect with the Spirit of God. The waystation calls an individual to reconsider their life at all levels by their encounter with an alternative reality.

Whether waystations are churches, para-church groups, small groups, house churches, web or blogsites, they need to be:

- Spaces and places which are easily located. Just as a Monarch butterfly on its migratory path must find food sources, so too must people of Christian faith. For this reason, waystations need to be accessible and welcoming to people.
- Spaces and places where people's stories and their community stories of truth and God are told and listened to. Here, people's stories can be heard as part of their journey, with respect and reverence.

- Spaces and places that leave room for discussion, differing views, alternative understandings and varied experiences.
- Spaces and places where sacred texts are engaged with and taken seriously as guides and encouragers.
- Spaces and places where deep wells of spirituality can be dug and shared rhythms of prayer and contemplation practiced.
- Spaces and places that evidence practical compassion for the marginalized, concern for social justice and give voice to the voiceless.
- Open spaces and places where wayfarers, like Monarch butterflies in migration, can belong for a few hours, days, months and where, for some, it can become their faith home. Spaces and places that know the longevity of any one person's stay is not as important as the influence of the waystation on them. For this reason waystations are not institutionally focused, but Spirit focused.
- Spaces and places where respect and reverence for another's journey is tangible.

Wayfarers and waystations are, I would suggest, crucial to the future of the church because the number of people exploring beyond a pre-critical faith is increasing due to the changing societal context of postmodern, post-Christian societies. George Barna has recently published a book called *Revolution: Finding Vibrant Faith Beyond The Walls Of The Sanctuary*, in which he suggests that the next great revolution in American Christianity is the revolution away from the church as the primary base for people's spiritual experience and expression. His research suggests that while in the year 2000 70 per cent of local Christians looked to the local church for their primary means of spiritual experience and expression, this number will drop to between 30–35 per cent by 2025. Correspondingly, while 5 per cent of Christians saw 'alternative faith-based community' as their primary means of spiritual experience and expression in 2000, this number will grow to 30–35 per cent by 2025. Barna goes on to comment on how people relate to these findings, saying, 'You don't have to like this transition, but you must deal with it. You can approach it with a defensive, negative attitude, or you can deal with it in the hope of learning and experiencing great breakthroughs in your life. That choice is yours.'[4] For those who are open to facing the coming changes, the journeys of individual wayfarers and waystations become models: models of hope.

As the 'Monarch Watch' people are calling for 10,000 waystations across America to feed migrating butterflies, I would want to call for tens of thousands of individuals, ministers, spiritual directors, small groups, blogsites, resource packs, books and church communities to be waystations for those on faith journeys beyond the known shapes of pre-critical Christian expression. In the rapidly changing culture, numerous waystations are needed. The fact is, we can no more predict or direct the faith explorations of individuals than we can predict and direct the migratory path of butterflies. There are tens of thousands of people who have experienced Christian faith as adults, who have been committed to it and actively involved in church communities and who now find themselves on solo migrations of faith. Some of these people are connected to churches; many are not. Either way, they need waystations: thousands of them, to nurture and feed them as they pass by.

Waystations are quite different to homes. Recently we hired a car and drove across southern Ireland. We enjoyed a fantastic few days of spring weather, breathtaking scenery and awe-inspiring historical sites. Each day, we opened the map and talked about where we wanted to go. Having devised a rough plan, we set off. If something caught our eye, we stopped. If a signpost or information sign pointed to somewhere that looked interesting, we went. When we felt hungry, we stopped and ate what we had with us or called into a country pub or local café. As the afternoon sun was sinking and evening beckoned, we would look for a bed and breakfast place to stop. There were hundreds of bed and breakfast places along the roads and, since we were not travelling in the tourist season, nearly all seemed to have vacancy signs. On more than one occasion we drove past four or five establishments and picked the one that looked like a place where we would like to stay. The next morning over coffee, we might ask the owner if there were any local spots worth savouring or for advice on how best to travel; and then, we were off again. We had no intention of living long-term at any of the places we stopped, yet we thoroughly enjoyed them as waystations on our journey.

In faith terms, waystations may be churches and Christian communities or groups for the people who have made them their home base; but, for many wayfarers (post-chrysalis faith people), they will be a place to alight, to be refreshed and then they will be beckoned on again. For those at the heart of these churches, communities and groups this can be hard to accept. People come and people go. The great majority will be here briefly or, at best, visit infrequently. If we are trying to build an institution rather than support individuals, we will inevitably find their transient nature discouraging. But being a waystation means having a bed and breakfast proprietor's mentality, rather than that of an institution builder.

12

Butterfly House – *beautifully hopeful*

An extension of the waystation is the 'butterfly house'. While waystations provide nectar to passing butterflies and swan plants for them to lay eggs on, 'butterfly houses' care for hundreds of different species of butterflies through all their life stages. They encourage growth in the number of butterflies, support research and provide an opportunity for people to see and enjoy a rich array of butterflies. In these places, small children, the elderly and adults alike can experience the fragile beauty of butterflies as they land on their arms, hands and shoulders. They can see the tiny caterpillars eating their way out of their skins and marvel at the different shapes and colours of the varying chrysalises. Such places are places of beauty and hope. In faith terms, they are signs of the kingdom of God.

Some butterfly houses are enclosed; others are open. An example of the latter is Butterfly Bay in a remote part of New Zealand. Butterfly Bay provides a rich habitat for butterflies with many host plants and a good climate. Here, tens of thousands of butterflies congregate, many eggs are laid and, as a result, numerous caterpillars and chrysalises are also to be found. In our rapidly changing society we need many butterfly houses of Christian faith. Sadly, the trend seems to be a move away from the richness, diversity and whole of faith approach in most churches.

As the Christian church moves into increasingly troubled and changing times, the journey into the desert places of faith is not only a journey undertaken by individuals but also by many church communities. Increasingly, we are seeing the churches in the west entering a new exile and darkness. The settled period of Christendom is crumbling and, with it, the structures and ways of church and the forms of faith that the Christendom model of church espoused. In our postmodern and post-Christendom contexts there appears to be a renewed focus from church leaders on theological conservatism and ecclesiological control. Put simply, church leaderships are circling the wagons against an increasingly chaotic and ever-changing culture.

I was speaking recently with two ministers who were lamenting recent decisions of their denomination on sexual ethics and theology. One summed up the cumulative shifts saying, 'It isn't the church that we joined.' The denomination had moved so far in ecclesiology, decision-making practice and theology towards conservatism and control that these two ministers felt sidelined, even unwanted. In the language of phases of faith, many church structures are strongly focusing on pre-critical faith expressions. They are encouraged to do this because this is the phase in which many people, especially young adults, come to faith. It is a style of church that can grow quickly as they can provide clear answers and beliefs, quick fixes to problems and a ready sense of belonging. But as denominations and churches increasingly focus on this phase of Christian faith, people who are moving beyond it into a critical phase of faith – a phase of faith characterized by questions, doubts, personal suffering and difficulty – find there is no room for them. Put simplistically, it is like a church saying we will focus on caterpillars. This is where the most growth is seen and where there is a correlation between the energy we put in and the growth we see. For caterpillars don't tend to wander far from their host plant and they are keen to consume: unlike the next stage, which is cocooned and individualistic. People in this chrysalis phase of faith do not need or want the faith diet that theologically and ecclesiologically conservative churches provide. And even more threatening is the faith equivalent of the butterfly phase: when people move quickly and easily between many Christian groups, are responsive to wider agendas than our own and don't have the same allegiance to a single church.

But for church leaders and communities willing to nurture people at all phases of the faith journey, the butterfly house may provide inspiration. There is hope and beauty in communities that take on a whole of faith approach with an acceptance of the loss of control this inevitably brings. There is something inherently rich about a community that can cater for the newest of Christians and the harshest of sceptics with mutual respect and understanding: where young and old, the sure and the unsure, caringly form community together. Butterfly houses provide such an environment for butterflies at every stage of their life cycle. Christian faith communities that model themselves on the butterfly houses are indications of the kingdom of God that Jesus spoke so much about.

Butterfly houses care for every stage of the life cycle. The people who run the butterfly houses understand each phase of the butterfly life cycle and with this knowledge they carefully nurture each stage, seeking to provide the food sources and contexts each stage needs.

People in the various phases of the faith journey need quite different support. It seems that they almost speak an incompatible language. So when those of pre-critical faith talk with post-critical faith people, the same words can have quite conflicting meanings and nuances. For those with a pre-critical faith, especially, this can be confusing. I had this experience yesterday. A man walked into the church building I work from and asked if we would like some tracts that he had produced and was giving away to churches for free. They were typical two-page Christian tracts focused on making a decision of faith and heavy on Scripture quotes. I had a look and thanked him for offering them, but said I doubted we would be able to use them. Somewhat surprised, he asked why, and I explained by giving him a copy of a welcome brochure we had produced. This brochure was pitched at people who had no idea of Christian faith or the Bible and might well be negatively disposed to the church. He then asked me the question, would I know where I was going if I died tonight? It is a question that irks me in its simplicity. I replied that I wouldn't know. I hoped that I would be with God,[1] but the best I knew was that 'the God of all eternity would do what is right' and the best I could do was to 'commit my spirit into God's hands'.

He looked a bit taken aback by my response and quoted a verse from Scripture about being sure of our salvation. I mentioned that from everything Jesus seemed to say about eternity, there were going to be many surprises but clearly, at some stage, 'God will be all in all'. Looking very perplexed, his next question was, 'Do you believe in the devil?' Realizing our experiences of Christian faith were poles apart and our conversation was only going to lead to more miscommunication I politely brought the conversation to a close. Clearly, we were not on the same wavelength. I was never going to fit comfortably within the faith formula in which he was trying to locate me, and he had no language with which to find me beyond his formula. I have little doubt he left concerned for my salvation and probably wrote me off as 'a liberal' or 'a heretic' or maybe as being 'deluded'.

Through my own journey of faith and through listening to the stories of others, I have slowly become aware of the different languages of the faith stages. As a pastor, this has been an enormously valuable tool. It is why I teach faith development courses and would want to see them as a mandatory part of all theological training. Being aware of the language people are using allows me to meet people where they are. It allows me to hear what is important to them and to respond in a way that is congruent with their phase of faith. It allows me to pray with people in a manner that gives an accompanying voice to their fears and needs. For me, it has become an extension of the command to weep with those who weep and laugh with those who laugh and is linked with the advice of Paul to be all things to all people in order to save some.[2]

Whenever we move into a new phase of faith, it is like becoming conversant in a new language. It takes a while and quite some learning and hard work but once the language is learned and we find ourselves conversant within it, we begin to enjoy the new world of culture and language it opens up for us. For St John of the Cross, it is in the darkness that we may sense God coming to us from a totally different direction and inviting us to learn to speak a new language. It seems that for a period of time God will only speak this new language to us, so that we may be immersed in it and learn to live comfortably within it and come to enjoy relating to God in this new and richer way. Later, we may find God speaking to us in both our old tongue and the new.

So, moving into a new faith phase does not mean we lose our understanding of the previous phase of faith or its language; we carry these within us. Just as people can be multilingual, people can, in faith stage terms, also be multi-stage. When multi-faith stage people confront a faith concern, dilemma or issue, they have, as it were, two or more languages with which to talk about it.

The idea that each new phase of faith is like learning a new language is helpful in understanding why people in different faith phases find it so hard to communicate together. James Fowler talks of 'cross-stage static' to explain the struggle that people of different faith stages have in understanding and valuing each other's faith expression. Post-critical faith sounds confusing for pre-critical faith people. It sounds very similar to what they believe, but it lacks the clarity they seek. When people from different faith phases interrelate, the core elements of their faith may be the same, for example the life, teaching, death and resurrection of Jesus Christ; yet, they are expressed and held in different ways.

The language of post-critical faith embraces people who don't fit within clear definitions and who seem less concerned with the boundaries that define pre-critical expressions of faith: the boundaries that define who is in and who is out.

A caution is needed here! The multi-language expression of our faith seems to come together only as we enter and become at home in a post-critical faith. The pre-critical and hyper-critical phases do not seem to join together until the post-critical becomes home base. In fact, in the hyper-critical phase of faith, there can often be an antipathy, even an anger, for pre-critical expressions of faith. Like oil and water, they do not mix without a third element that can unite them and hold them together. This third element is the journey into a post-critical expression of faith.

Learning to listen to and appreciate the different phases of faith not only calls for an understanding of how Christian faith typically develops, but also a respect for people in each phase. It demands tolerance and grace. For those who have travelled furthest, I believe there is a necessity to show grace to those who have travelled less. Pre-critical people cannot understand post-critical people any more than a caterpillar can understand or imagine itself as a butterfly. But the reverse is not true; because of this, those who have travelled furthest must show grace and compassion. I believe this wholeheartedly and it disturbs me to see such grace being abused in some of the controversial ethical situations facing the church today, as those with a pre-critical stance expect their view to be adopted without offering any inclusion for other perspectives.

This is where the 'butterfly house' comes to the fore. We desperately need churches, communities and conversations where people of the different phases of Christian faith can come together to recognize the uniqueness of their own faith expression, learn to appreciate that their way is not the only way and learn how to respect each other. What makes visiting the butterfly house such a rich experience is seeing all the varieties and stages of butterflies brought together. Here, pupae, caterpillars, chrysalises and butterflies can all be seen together. The Christian faith in western societies desperately needs to multiply the places where the richness of diversity can be expressed; it needs places and spaces where people of different phases of faith can learn from each other. In James Fowler's analysis of the stages of faith, he points to both the strengths and weaknesses of each stage. All the stages have potential vulnerable areas, the only cure for which is being in continual conversation with the strengths of the other stages.

Not only do we need waystations that will support individuals with a deep theology and a post-critical faith expression, we also need 'butterfly houses'; we need spaces and places where people of all phases of faith can come together. We need places where the breadth of the Christian journey can be celebrated, where raw beginners can hear the wisdom in the stories of those who have travelled far in the Christian faith and where those who have travelled far can be encouraged by the passion and conviction of raw beginners. In these spaces and places fundamentalist agendas can be softened and the diversity and richness of the Christian faith can be seen and experienced by the wider community.

End Notes

1. Butterflies – *transformation*

1   See www.chrysalis.ie
2   From a research perspective see A. Jamieson, *A Churchless Faith: Faith Journeys Beyond The Churches* (London: SPCK, 2002) and A. Jamieson, J. McIntosh, A. Thompson, *Church Leavers: Faith journeys five years on* (London: SPCK, 2006), and from a pastoral perspective, A. Jamieson, *Journeying in Faith: In and Beyond the Tough Places* (London: SPCK, 2004).
3   K. Stokes, *Faith is a Verb: Dynamics of Adult Faith Development* (Mystic, Connecticut: Twenty-Third Publications, 1992), 4.
4   1 Cor. 13:11; Heb. 5:12; 1 Cor. 3:2. Compare with Jn. 4:34 to see the solid food Jesus chose.
5   Frederick Buechner, in W. Zinsser (ed.) *Going on Faith* (Marlowe & Company, 1999) cited by Philip Yancey, *Soul Survivor: How My Faith Survived the Church* (Hodder & Stoughton, 2001²), 242.
6   See the best-seller: Victor Frankyl, *Man's Search for Meaning* (New York: Pocket Books, a division of Simon & Schuster, Inc., 2004).
7   Sharon Parks, *The Critical Years: The Young Adults Search for a Faith to Live by* (San Francisco: Harper & Row, 1986), XV.
8   Cited in: Rosemary Broughton, *Praying with Teresa of Avila* (Minnesota: Saint Mary's Press, 1990), 47–48.
9   Erik H. Erikson, *The Life Cycle Completed* (New York: W.W. Norton & Company, 1997), 59.

2. Can't Get Enough – *growing*

[1] Jack R. Pressau, *I'm Saved, You're Saved – Maybe* (Atlanta, GA: John Knox Press, 1977).

[2] Thomas H. Green, S.J., *When the Well Runs Dry: Prayer Beyond the Beginnings* (Notre Dame, Indiana: Ave Maria Press, 1998), 46.

[3] Cited in Thomas H. Green, S.J., *When the Well Runs Dry: Prayer Beyond the Beginnings*, 42–43.

3. Golden Crucible – *cocooning*

[1] A. Jamieson, *Called Again: In and beyond the deserts of faith* (Wellington: Philip Garside Publishing, 2004) and *Journeying in Faith: In and Beyond the Tough Places*.

[2] Gerald May, *The Dark Night of the Soul: A Psychiatrist Explores the Connection Between Darkness and Spiritual Growth* (New York: HarperSanFrancisco, 2004), 90–91.

[3] First published in A. Jamieson, 'Should I stay or should I go: Understanding some church leavers' *Canvas Magazine*, Issue 4, 1st Quarter 1997, 4–6.

[4] Drawn from the research of Sharon Parks, *The Critical Years: The Young Adults Search for a Faith to Live by*, XXX.

[5] David Lyon, *Postmodernity* (Milton Keynes: Open University Press, 1994), 11.

[6] Here, I am drawing on a number of sociologists and linking their respective work under these five headings.

[7] The fall of bureaucratic state socialism.

[8] David Lyon, *Postmodernity* 27.

[9] Philosophically, many base the modern period on Decartes' statement, *'Cognito ergo sum'* – I think therefore I am.

[10] This is the metaphor used by David Lyon (*Postmodernity* [Minnesota: Open University Press, 1994], and, more extensively by Zygmunt Bauman in his description of modern society as 'Liquid Modernity'. Bauman uses the image of fluids that 'travel easily . . . flow, spill, run out, splash, pour over, leak, flood, spray, drip, seep and ooze' (*Liquid Modernity* [Cambridge: Polity Press, 2000 p. 2]), in contrast to solids which are fixed, dependable and stable. He argues that the solids of modernity are being liquefied, not so they can be re-formed into new solid

structures but, so they can remain perpetually in fluid motion. This process of the 'melting of the solids' of modernity has led to a loss of the old foundations, of order, of structures and of systems. John Ralston Saul extends this image further as he talks of 'civilization being in a long term crisis, "drifting further out into a cold, unfriendly, confusing sea". Change is happening faster than we can understand or manage and if we are to ride out such bewildering and destructive times, we need to have the self-awareness and flexibility that resilience brings (cited in *Resilience* [Deveson, A., Sydney: Allen & Unwin, 2003, p. 10]).'

11 Pete Ward, *Liquid Church* (Carlisle: Paternoster, 2002).

12 Len Sweet (ed.) *Perfect Storm* – to be published 2007, Darryl Dash is cited at http://www.dashhouse.com/darryl/2006/03/navigating_the.htm. They draw on an actual storm front, created by three storm fronts colliding together, that hit the United States and formed the basis of the film *The Perfect Storm*.

13 Cited in Anne Deveson, *Resilience* (Crows Nest: Allen & Unwin, 2003), 18.

14 Anne Deveson, *Resilience*, 19.

15 Alan Jones, *Soul Making: The Desert Way of Spirituality* (San Francisco: HarperCollins, 1989), 22.

16 Kester Brewin, *The Complex Christ: Signs of Emergence in the Urban Church* (London: SPCK Publishing, 2004), 15.

17 http://lesstravelled.net/2005/09/07/oh-dear/.

18 The Greek word is χρυσοξ

4. In the Dark – *accompanying*

1 Mike Riddell, *Godzone: A Traveller's Guide* (Oxford: Lion Publishing, 1992), 43.

2 Gerald May, *The Dark Night of the Soul: A Psychiatrist Explores the Connection Between Darkness and Spiritual Growth*, 67.

3 Mt. 11:28–30, Eugene H. Petersen, *The Message* (Colorado Springs: NavPress, 1993).

4 Karen Armstrong, *The Spiral Staircase: A Memoir* (London: Harper Perennial, 2005), 301–302.

5 The word 'liminal' from the Latin *limen* (threshold), was first used by the anthropologist Arnold van Gennep. The liminal signifies the in-between time. Arnold van Gennep described it as like the neutral zone that often existed between nations

in antiquity. He described these zones as often being deserts, marshes or virgin forest where everyone had full rights to travel and hunt.

6 Gerald May, *The Dark Night of the Soul*, 96.

7 I. Matthew, *The Impact of God: Soundings from St John of The Cross* (London: Hodder & Stoughton, 1995), 16.

8 Jn. 1:5 (GNB).

9 Parker Palmer, *Let Your Life Speak: Listening for the Voice of Vocation* (San Francisco: Jossey-Bass, 2000), 87.

10 Henri Nouwen, *Life of the Beloved: Spiritual Living in a Secular World* (New York: Crossroad Publishing Company, 1992), 33, 43.

11 Henri Nouwen, *Life of the Beloved*, 62.

12 Henri Nouwen, *Life of the Beloved*, 77.

13 Henri Nouwen, *Life of the Beloved*, 62.

14 Henri Nouwen, *Life of the Beloved*, 83–84.

15 Henri Nouwen, *Life of the Beloved*, 55.

16 Parker Palmer, *Let Your Life Speak*, 88.

17 Parker Palmer, *Let Your Life Speak*, 89.

18 Parker Palmer, *Let Your Life Speak*, 90.

19 Parker Palmer, *Let Your Life Speak*, 85.

20 Taken from my notes of lectures in a series on suffering, Easter and hope that include this saying of Von Balthasar in Mysterium Paschale.

21 See Mt. 8:31; 16:21; 17:23; Mk. 8:31; 9:31; Lk. 17:25.

22 Mt. 27:46 (CEV).

23 The Apostles' Creed states: '. . . was crucified, dead, and buried. He descended into hell.' God extended compassion to the dead in sheol in Christ's descent into hell but that does not remove the freedom of choice given to each person. For surely the great gift of God to humanity is freedom to choose

24 Daniel O'Leary, 'In Lent we grow by dying', *Tui Motu InterIslands*, April 2007, 24–25.

25 See Gen. 32:22–32.

26 Pierre Teilhard de Chardin, *The Divine Milieu: An Essay on the Interior Life* (New York: Harper, 1957), 62.

27 Parker Palmer, *Let Your Life Speak*, 95.

28 A New Zealand Prayer Book / He Karakia Mihinare o Aotearoa. Gratefully used here with permission.

5. From Deep Within – *letting go*

1   Jn. 15:15.
2   Paul Tillich, http://prodigal.typepad.com/prodigal_
    kiwi/2007/01/index.html
3   Dietrich Bonhoeffer, *The Cost of Discipleship* (London: SCM Press,
    1955), 38-9.
4   Karen Armstrong, *The Spiral Staircase*, 15 and 75.
5   Gerald May, *The Dark Night of the Soul*, 126–127.
6   Harrison Owen, *The Power of Spirit: How Organizations Transform*
    (San Francisco: Berrett-Koehler Publishers Inc, 2000), 91.
7   Harrison Owen, *The Power of Spirit*, 92.

6. Being Alongside – *accompanying*

1   A. Jamieson, J. McIntosh, A. Thompson, *Church Leavers* (London:
    SPCK, 2006).
2   Daniel O'Leary, 'In Lent we grow by dying', *Tui Motu Interislands*,
    April 2007, 24–25.
3   These groups were developed as part of Spirited Exchanges.
    Information about the groups and other initiatives of Spirited
    Exchanges is available at www.spiritedexchanges.org.nz or
    www.spiritedexchanges.org.uk
4   Doug Reichel, 'Thoughts on the desert walk', *Stimulus*, February
    1994, 2:1, 11–16.
5   There are many good websites with lists of the signs and
    symptoms of depression.
6   Gerald May, *The Dark Night of the Soul*, 158.

7. Going Solo – *emergence*

1   Fredrick Buechner, *Wishful Thinking: A Seeker's ABC* (San
    Francisco: HarperSanFrancisco, 1993), 119.
2   Cited in: Parker Palmer, *Let Your Life Speak*, 16–17.
3   Parker Palmer, *Let Your Life Speak*, 10.
4   Parker Palmer, *Let Your Life Speak*, 7–8.
5   Sharon Parks, *The Critical Years*, 88.
6   Parker Palmer, *The Company of Strangers: Christians and the
    Renewal of America's Public Life* (New York: Crossroad Publishing
    Company, 1985), 43.

7 Thomas H. Green, S.J., *Drinking from a Dry Well* (Notre Dame, Indiana: Ave Maria Press, 1991), 26–27.
8 1 Cor. 13:13.
9 James Twyman, *The Prayer of St Francis* (Scotland: Findhorn Press, 2002) 36-40.

8. Imago – *being*

1 Sharon Parks, *The Critical Years,* 50.
2 Italics added for clarity.
3 Sharon Parks, *The Critical Years,* 50.
4 Later, a posthumous retrial would exonerate her and lay the path to her later canonization as a saint.
5 Cited in: Parker Palmer, *Let Your Life Speak,* 11.
6 Cited in: Parker Palmer *Let Your Life Speak,* 25.
7 Elisabeth Moltmann-Wendell, 'Self-Love and Self-acceptance' in *Love the Foundation of Hope: The Theology of Jurgen Moltmann and Elisabeth Moltmann-Wendell* F.B. Burnham & C.S. McCoy et al. (eds.) (San Francisco: Harper & Row, 1988), 26.
8 Words in square brackets are mine.
9 Elisabeth Moltmann-Wendell, 'Self-love and Self-acceptance' in *Love the Foundation of Hope: The Theology of Jurgen Moltmann* and *Elisabeth Moltmann-Wendell* F.B. Burnham & C.S. McCoy et al. (eds.), 37.
10 Richard Rohr, 'The spirituality of the two halves of life', *Tui Motu InterIslands*, December 2006, 19.

9. Butterfly Effect – *flying*

1 Gerald May, *The Dark Night of the Soul,* 88.

10. Looking Back – *seeing the whole*

1 Paul Ricoeur, *The Symbolism of Evil* (New York: Harper Row, 1967), 349.
2 Briege O'Hare, 'Opening to Love: A Paradigm for Growth in Relationship with God' in *Spiritual Direction*, vol. 10, no. 2, June 2004, 27–36.
3 Here, Brueggemann alludes to 1 Cor 13:7.

4 Walter Brueggemann, *The Psalms and the Life of Faith* (Minneapolis: Augsburg Fortress, 1995), 25.

5 J.O. Hagberg and R.A. Guelich, *The Critical Journey: Stages in the Life of Faith* (Dallas: Word Publishing, 1989).

6 Gerald May, *The Dark Night of the Soul*, 130.

7 Philip Richter and Leslie Francis, *Gone But Not Forgotten* (London: Darton, Longman and Todd, 1998), 53.

11. Monarch Waystations – *being strategic*

1 See www.monarchwatch.org.

2 See A. Jamieson, *Journeying in Faith*.

3 See A. Jamieson, *A Churchless Faith*.

4 George Barna, *Revolution: Finding Vibrant Faith Beyond The Walls Of The Sanctuary* (Wheaton: Tyndale, 2005), 49–50.

12. Butterfly House – *beautifully hopeful*

1 For me hope is a wisdom of the heart that carries enormous gravity because it is based on the lived trust in the promises of God.

2 Rom. 12:15 and 1 Cor. 9:22

Series Titles Currently Available

Atonement for a 'Sinless' Society
Engaging with an emerging culture

Atonement for a 'Sinless' Society

Engaging with an Emerging Culture

Alan Mann

'Sin doesn't really exist as a serious idea in modern life,' wrote the journalist Bryan Appleyard. He is not alone in his views. 'Sin' has become just as tainted, polluted and defiled in the postmodern mind as the word itself indicates.

Atonement for a 'Sinless' Society is about an encounter between two stories: the story of the postmodern, post-industrialized, post-Christian 'sinless' self and the story of atonement played out in the Passion Narrative. Alan Mann charts a way through the apparent impasse between a story that supposedly relies on sin and guilt to become meaningful, and one that fails to recognize the plight of humanity as portrayed in this way. He shows how the biblical narrative needs to be reread in the light of this emerging story so that it can speak meaningfully and sufficiently to an increasingly 'sinless' society.

'Clear, creative, deep, compelling and inspiring' – **Brian D. McLaren**, author, speaker, networker

'Alan Mann's voice is needed and welcome . . . A penetrating analysis of the world we inhabit.' – **Joel B. Green**, Asbury Theological Seminary

'An insightful, timely and creative view of the atonement for our postmodern times.' – **Steve Chalk**, Oasis Trust

978-1-84227-355-5

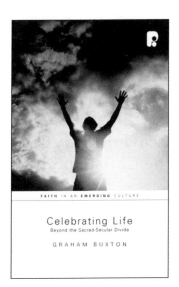

Celebrating Life
Beyond the Sacred-Secular Divide
GRAHAM BUXTON

Celebrating Life

Beyond the Sacred-Secular Divide

Graham Buxton

As Christians, our engagement with the world and with culture is often impoverished as a result of unbiblical dualisms. More than we realise, the divide between sacred and secular is reinforced in our minds, contributing to an unhealthy and, at times, narrow super-spirituality. Seeking a more postmodern, holistic and, ultimately, more *Christian* approach to culture, Graham Buxton leads us on a journey towards the celebration of life in *all* its dimensions.

The first part of the book examines the roots of our dualistic thinking and its implications for culture. Part Two draws us from dualism to holism in a number of chapters that consider our engagement with literature, the creative arts, science, politics and business. Part Three draws the threads together by setting out the dimensions of a more holistic theology of the church's engagement with, and participation in, contemporary society that will lead us 'beyond the sacred-secular divide'.

> 'This is incarnational theology at its best!' – **Ray S. Anderson**, Senior Professor of Theology and Ministry, Fuller Theological Seminary, California.

Graham Buxton is Director of Postgraduate Studies in Ministry and Theology, Tabor College, Adelaide, Australia. He is author of Dancing in the Dark and The Trinity, Creation and Pastoral Ministry.

978-1-84227-507-1

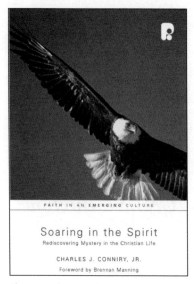

Soaring in the Spirit

Rediscovering Mystery in the Christian Life

Charles J. Conniry, Jr.

This is a book about experiencing the presence of Jesus Christ in the moment-by-moment 'nows' of daily life. James McClendon, Jr. observed that the first task of theology is to locate our place in the story. Like finding directions at a shopping mall with the brightly coloured words, 'you are here,' the author invites us into an encounter with the 'we-are-here' place in God's Great Story. The claim of this book is that the experience of Christ's presence in the 'right-here' of our daily walk – *Christian soaring* – is the birthright of every follower of Jesus Christ. This is a thoughtful, stirring, and ground-breaking book on the neglected topic of *Christian soaring through discerning discipleship*.

> 'This book is a *tour de force* . . . and can be read with profit by believers and unbelievers, philosophers and theologians, pastors and lay people, and anyone who longs to soar in the Spirit . . . It not only blessed me but drew me to prayer.' – **Brennan Manning**, author of *The Ragamuffin Gospel*.

Charles J. Conniry, Jr. is Associate Professor of Pastoral Ministry and Director of the Doctor of Ministry Program at George Fox Evangelical Seminary, Portland.

978-1-84227-508-5

Re:Mission

Biblical Mission for a Post-Biblical Church

Andrew Perriman

In this innovative and radical book postmodern mission and New Testament studies collide. Andrew Perriman examines the mission of the earliest church in its historical context and argues that our context is very different and *so our mission cannot simply be a matter of doing exactly what the earliest church did.* The key question at the heart of the book is, 'How do we shape a *biblical* theology of mission for a *post-biblical* church?'

> '*Re:Mission* distinguishes Perriman as a scholar who must be reckoned with in this time of rethinking and transition. A great piece of work!' – **Brian D. McLaren**, author (brianmclaren.net)

> 'Andrew Perriman has addressed one of the most challenging facets of New Testament teaching and he does so with remarkable insight and creativity. This fascinating book makes for urgent reading.' – **Craig A. Evans**, Payzant Distinguished Professor of New Testament, Acadia Divinity College, Canada

Andrew Perriman lives in Holland and works with Christian Associates seeking to develop open, creative communities of faith for the emerging culture in Europe. He is author of *Speaking of Women* about Paul's teaching on women, *Faith, Health and Prosperity*, and, *The Coming of the Son of Man: New Testament Eschatology for an Emerging Church.*

978-1-84227-545-0

Forthcoming Series Title

Metavista:
Bible, Church and Mission in an Age of Imagination
COLIN GREENE & MARTIN ROBINSON
the church after postmodernity

Metavista

Bible, Church and Mission in an Age of Imagination

Colin Green and Martin Robinson

The core narrative of the Christian faith, the book that conveys it (the Bible) and the institution of the church have all been marginalised by the development of modernity and post-modernity. Strangely, post-modernity has created an opportunity for religious thinking and experience to re-enter the lives of many. Yet, despite its astonishing assault on modernity, post-modernity is not itself an adequate framework for thinking about life. There is therefore a new opportunity for Christians to imagine what comes *after* post-modernity and to prepare the church, its book and its story for a new engagement of mission with western culture. The church on the margins, through a creative missionary imagination can audaciously re-define the centre of western cultural life. This book will attempt to sketch what such an approach might look like

> 'If you have a taste for the subversive, a passion for the church, a heart for biblical engagement, and an eye on the future; this book is a must-read.'
> – **Roy Searle**, Northumbria Community, former President of the Baptist Union of Great Britain

Colin Greene is Professor of Theological and Cultural Studies at Mars Hill Graduate School in Seattle. He is author of *Christology in Cultural Perspective*.

Martin Robinson is an international speaker, a writer, and Director of 'Together in Mission'.

978-1-84227-506-1